T0316515

Cambridge Elements ≡

Elements in the Economics of Emerging Markets
edited by
Bruno S. Sergi
Harvard University

LATIN AMERICA GLOBAL INSERTION, ENERGY TRANSITION, AND SUSTAINABLE DEVELOPMENT

Leonardo E. Stanley
Centre for the Study of State and Society (CEDES)

CAMBRIDGE
UNIVERSITY PRESS

CAMBRIDGE
UNIVERSITY PRESS

University Printing House, Cambridge CB2 8BS, United Kingdom

One Liberty Plaza, 20th Floor, New York, NY 10006, USA

477 Williamstown Road, Port Melbourne, VIC 3207, Australia

314–321, 3rd Floor, Plot 3, Splendor Forum, Jasola District Centre,
New Delhi – 110025, India

79 Anson Road, #06–04/06, Singapore 079906

Cambridge University Press is part of the University of Cambridge.

It furthers the University's mission by disseminating knowledge in the pursuit of
education, learning, and research at the highest international levels of excellence.

www.cambridge.org
Information on this title: www.cambridge.org/9781108809986
DOI: 10.1017/9781108893398

First published 2020

A catalogue record for this publication is available from the British Library.

ISBN 978-1-108-80998-6 Paperback
ISSN 2631–8598 (online)
ISSN 2631-858X (print)

Latin America Global Insertion, Energy Transition, and Sustainable Development

Elements in the Economics of Emerging Markets

DOI: 10.1017/9781108893398
First published online: November 2020

Leonardo E. Stanley
Centre for the Study of State and Society (CEDES)
Author for correspondence: lstanley@cedes.org

Abstract: This Element focuses on Latin American fossil fuel producer countries and how they are dealing with the transition towards a greener energy matrix. The challenges involved are multiple and ethical in substance. In particular, a worldwide expansion in clean energies would reduce climate change's, physical risks. A rapid transition, however, induces the irruption of a new (financial) risk. The energy transition, in addition, could be thought of as a new arena for political disputes. Finally, it evaluates the relevance of monetary policy and financial regulation to tackle the issue from a macro perspective. Energy transition, however, also has long-term but uncertain consequences on the national economy. Therefore, and in order to minimize risks, a long-term, strategic vision of the challenge confronted by the region becomes mandatory. To tackle all these problems, this Element profits from the contributions of different disciplines.

Keywords: Latin American economies, energy transition, climate change, finance, inequality, carbon markets, macroeconomics, development

ISBNs: 9781108809986 (PB), 9781108893398 (OC)
ISSNs: 2631-8598 (online), ISSN 2631-858X (print)

Contents

1 Introduction

This Element focuses on Latin American fossil fuel producer countries and how they are dealing with the transition towards a greener energy matrix. Since the late nineteenth century, the provision of energy has been an essential aspect of life, with fossil fuels a determining factor in the economic development process. The benefits of fossil fuel adoption, however, ignored the high cost that its exploitation imposed on the environment. In the 1970s, critical voices began alerting how the "empty world" model was reaching its limits (Meadows et al., 1972). The idea of sustainable development emerged, initially embodied in the "Our Future in Common" report issued by the United Nations Commission for Environment and Development in 1987 (WCED, 1987). From then on, the sustainability ideal gained acceptance. Years later, the British government entrusted Nicholas Stern with a special report, which would put climate change and global warming at the forefront of the debate (Stern, 2007). [1] After observing the increase in temperatures, the accelerating melting of glaciers, and the rising sea level, a group of experts from the Inter-Governmental Panel on Climate Change (IPCC) concluded that the warming of the land is irrefutable (IPPC, 2007).

The climate emergency is with us; nobody could scientifically deny this (Ripple et al., 2020). The challenges ahead are many, indeed. Recent research has revealed that the Earth's nine boundaries are close to their limit with most of them exceeding the lower levels (Steffen et al., 2015). [2] We are entering into a highly insecure and risky area, which, for climate change, operates in a range of emissions between 350 and 450 parts per million (ppm). It crossed the lower limit in 1995, to establish a new record of 415 ppm (as of May 2019). [3] If this process continues, it would lead to an increase in the global temperature of over 4.0 °C by the end of this century.

In addition, there is the presence of specific tipping points, the surpassing of which might bring unimaginable consequences for global weather, triggering multiple chain reactions (Scheffer et al., 2001; Lenton et al., 2008). All these facts, in sum, are calling for immediate action. During the twenty-first

---

[1] According to the UFCC article 1, climate change is understood as: "a change of climate which is attributed directly or indirectly to human activity that alters the composition of the global atmosphere and which is in addition to natural climate variability observed over comparable time period."

[2] The nine boundaries or "ecological ceilings" refers to climate change, biosphere loss, land-system change, freshwater use, biochemical flows, ocean acidification, air pollution, ozone layer depletion, and novel entities (Steffen et al., 2015).

[3] According to figures from the global atmospheric carbon dioxide concentration measured at Mauna Loa Observatory in Hawaii, and reported by the Scripps Institution of Oceanography at UC San Diego. See https://scripps.ucsd.edu/programs/keelingcurve.

Conference of the Parties (COP) of the United Nations Framework Convention on Climate Change (UNFCC) (Paris, November–December 2015), UN members reached a historic agreement that seeks to prevent a 2.0 °C rise in global temperature for the remainder of the century and contain it at 1.5 °C. The ultimate goal of the agreement is to achieve a zero-emission level by 2050, with some governments proposing to accomplish that goal by 2030 (https://eciu .net/netzerotracker).

The signatory countries committed themselves to the so-called, nationally determined contributions (NDCs). Set every five years, NDCs involve unconditional (to local funding) as well as conditioned (to external financing) actions from each of the signatories. However, despite the highly ambitious commitments made, real efforts are falling short (Stigliz and Stern, 2017; Nordhaus, 2020), including those emanating from Latin America (ECLAC, 2018). Climate change is already impacting daily life and future generations face substantial consequences if the status quo prevails. The magnitude of the physical risks remains unknown, but the economic hazards and financial risks continue to build up.

Fossil fuels release carbon particles (CO_2) into the atmosphere, where their continuous presence (stock) explains the greenhouse accumulation problem (63 percent of total emissions are related to fuels). Henceforth, and to reduce risks and mitigate impacts, the scientific community proposed reducing the use of fossil fuels – including the rapid phasing out of coal. To maintain a temperature increase below 2 °C, the IPCC proposes a budget of 870–1,240 Gt CO_2 for the period 2011–50, proposing to keep one third of proved oil reserves unburned and half of the gas reserves in the ground (McGlade and Ekins, 2015, Friends of the Earth, 2017; Verkuijl, 2018). This leads to the concept of "carbon budget," which also infers the amount of oil, gas, and mineral coal that can be extracted by 2050. However, moving from an economy anchored in fossil fuels to another on renewable energy is not simple. On the one hand, the transition shows a non-linear dynamic trend. On the other hand, the process exceeds the technological sphere to involve institutional, political, and social aspects. Transition, in short, conveys a highly complex task for policymakers.

The issue of climate change has received considerable critical attention and numerous contributions have emerged aiming to support the sustainable development ideal. The challenges involved in the transition are multiple and ethical in substance. First, the problem of intertemporal justice is that mitigation benefits future generations, whereas the present should bear the costs. Next, the inter-generational problem, as the transition costs are often on the shoulders of less-favored sectors. Last but not least, the North–South divide, as current, accumulated levels of emissions associate with a small group of countries. The challenges are formidable, but their resolution goes beyond technical considerations.

As a result of these challenges, a group of scholars starts to work on the design of a new financial scheme, which evenly responds to the expectations of present and future generations. Academics have also started to accentuate economic and social-political interactions, particularly relevant at the designing of the energy transition path. If correctly designed, the move towards a new technological paradigm "can help countries meet their policy goals for secure, reliable and affordable energy; electricity access for all; reduced price volatility; and the promotion of social and economic development".

The new energy paradigm presents opportunities for less developed, energy-dependent countries (IRENA, 2019b). First, availability: in contrast to fossil fuels, RE is present almost everywhere. Second, fluidity: RE comes as a flow, difficult to stock although storage capacity is improving (and fast). Next, scale: RE could be produced in small units (mega-watts) by cooperatives or in large units (giga-watts) by traditional firms. Finally, almost nil marginal costs but high upfront costs (now diminishing). Altogether, these characteristics hamper dependence from foreign sources. Hydroelectricity is an essential source of energy in Latin America,[4] with generation close to 100 percent clean in countries like Paraguay, Costa Rica, Uruguay, or Chile. Renewables are less critical as secondary sources, or energy for direct consumption: transport, industry, households. For oil and gas producers, sustainability ideals clash with the sovereign desire for new rents. Physical availability, however, should be contrasted with economic accessibility. Most fossil fuels in Latin America require more sophisticated technology and, thus, a higher price than in other regions of the world, making the region even more vulnerable to energy price shocks than other fossil fuel producers.

What follows is an account of the challenges posed by energy transition in the region, with particular attention on the fossil fuel exporters. In Section 2, we evaluate the inter-temporal dimension of climate change interrelation, and the need for a new, common good approach in finance. Section 3 analyzes the various economic–social challenges arising at the transition, particularly stressing the issue of intra-generational equity. A summary of the main macroeconomic–developmental challenges, alongside the strategic perspective, is introduced in Section 4. In Section 5, we introduce some concluding remarks.

---

[4] South America concentrates 25 percent of the world's hydroelectric potential. Fifty-five percent of the electricity of the region generates from renewable energy, more than double the world average (22 percent). Davalos, Victorio Oxilio (2012). Matriz Energética en América Latina y el Caribe, Situación Actual y Perspectivas de la Energías Renovables. Organización Latino Americana de Energía – OLADE PPT Presentación – La Habana, www.olade.org/sites/default/files/presentaciones-sej/8_Presentación%20OLADE%20UPADI%20201.pdf.

2 Finances for the Common Good

Latin America is often portrayed as a natural paradise. Its mountains, plateaus, rivers, and seas house 40 percent of the world's biodiversity, 30 percent of global freshwater and almost 50 percent of tropical forests. At the same time, the region is rich in minerals and hydrocarbons. The magic and the spell, all in the same continent, blessed and cursed alike. So, although environmental problems are long-standing, the threat of global warming is recent. Moreover, despite how unfair the situation might be, the region can be strongly affected by climate change (ECLAC, 2014b; Hansen and Sato, 2016).

Climate change is associated with the emergence of new physical risks, which will have an impact on the national economy. Unequivocally, the situation shows us the convenience of moving towards renewables sources, but the process is far from being risk-free. There is always an impact on the economy, since the transition to a society with "low carbon combustion" implies simultaneous creation and destruction. The future will be uncertain and risky, but the status quo is certainly not an option. Hence, what is needed is to make "financial flows consistent with a pathway of low-carbon emission and climate-resilient development" (Stiglitz and Stern, 2017, page 6).

Financial funds move freely around the world, instantly and with no restrictions. Immediacy is facilitated by multiple factors, including technological advancements and financial deregulation. Technology guarantees the rational and utilitarian agent the immediacy of the return, whereas the current institutional framework validates such temporal-spatial configuration. To finance the transition to a 1.5-degree world, we need a different system to come out. In this sense, a new financial order should reveal "the likely future cost of business and payment for emissions" (Carney, 2019).

The move from the (short-term, profit maximization) financial return in favor of a new, sustainable (long-term, common good) concept (Schoenmaker and Schramade, 2019; Vercelli, 2019), implies abandoning firms' narrow vision and moving away from the current approach directed to short-term profitability (Section 2.1). In the search for an alternative financial model, one that fits with the sustainable development ideal, it is necessary to redefine incentives, rules, and practices lest inaction expose investors to massive losses in a not-too-distant future. A rapid transition, however, adds uncertainty and introduces a new financial risk (Section 2.2.a). Maintaining the current investment pattern could increase the financial costs of any future transition path (Section 2.2.b). Many countries have already started the process of transforming the electricity sector, involving different financial mechanisms. In the electricity-generation domain, governments are mostly using two different schemes: public auctions and feed-in-tariff (FIT) mechanisms (Section 2.3).

2.1 Traditional Finance and the Financing of the Common Good

When analyzing the viability of a project, investors only observe the rate of return. It is all that matters, as they detach themselves from the social and environmental consequences generated by the project. As social inequalities continue to deepen and an increasing number of environmental-related catastrophes emerge, opposition to traditional finance has started to emerge. A multidisciplinary vision has become commonplace, and the new theory of finance is moving towards long-term value creation.

Objections to the traditional vision are not just found in academic circles, but are increasingly coming from business groups and investment funds (ACCA, 2016; Dyllick and Muff, 2017; Hart and Zingales, 2017; CPI, 2019).[5] A new, more inclusive perspective is also permeating the judiciary, and not just confined to developed countries' courts (Cardoso, 2015; Samaniego et al., 2017) or even to international instances.[6] A more cautious, pro-environmental approach permeates the insurance industry (Bank of England, 2015; BIS, 2019), with an increasing number of companies refusing to bring insurance to (or pricing a premium on) carbon-related companies.[7] In other words, the new vision comes to challenge the traditional foundations of finance.

Climate change confronts authorities with a more daunting challenge related to the inter-temporal nature of the problem. The rise in global temperatures responds to emissions from burning carbon in the past (stock) and current burning (flow) induces a further increase in temperature in the future. Mark Carney (2015) describes this problem as "the tragedy of the horizon."

In dealing with this problem, mainstream finance theory presents several methodological disadvantages. One major drawback is that it adopts an a-temporal and a-space framework, which leads to a short-term bias. More misleading are the assumptions made by the model: rational investors, no information problems, and perfect and efficient markets. Under such circumstances, share prices reflect all available information; all risks are fully revealed.

---

[5] From a broader perspective, there is a consensus that market and company short-termism reduces economic efficiency, contributes to asset price bubbles, and lowers investor returns.

[6] The case of the Kichwa Indigeous People of Sarayak vs Ecuador, at the Inter-American Courts of Human Rights, www.corteidh.or.cr/docs/casos/articulos/seriec_245_ing.pdf.

[7] Scott Carpenter, "Axa's vow to stop insuring coal hits at industry's soft underbelly," Forbes. November 30, 2019. Julia Kolewe "Coal power becoming 'uninsurable' as firms refuse cover," The Guardian. December 2, 2019.

BOX 1 A FRAMEWORK FOR SUSTAINABLE FINANCE

The idea of sustainable financing involves a different type of firm, one that internalizes all negative environmental or social externalities generated by the activity. Despite everything, it is difficult – fortunately not impossible – to make entrepreneurs assume externalities (San Sebastian and Hurtiz, 2004, Sinnot et al., 2010; Zarsky and Stanley, 2013; Zarsky, 2014; Cardoso, 2015; Dyllick and Muff, 2017; Hart and Zingales, 2017; Shapira and Zingales, 2017). Business behavior responds to the government's inability to introduce adequate legislation or, if regulation exists, to properly enforce it (Tienhaara, 2009; Cardoso, 2015; Stanley, 2020). This permissive behavior is widely extended and due to multiple reasons, a practice largely observed among Latin American firms.

The cases being introduced exemplify how academia treated social and environmental concerns, how society's views influenced the archetypical vision of the firm, and how regulation has historically evolved (Table 1).

The traditional oil firm only envisions maximizing shareholder value: this is the vision behind M. Friedman's (1970) "business of business is business" motto (F). In the Ecuadorian Amazon region, Texaco's behavior offers an example of the pre-environmentally conscious age, where a firm's damages and pollution benefited from public disinterest (i.e., unregulated business). With environmental activism on the rise after the Rio Conference, corporate leaders started to moderate their discourse. Around the same time, Latin America decided to forego the Import Substitution Industrialization (ISI) model and to embrace the natural resources export model.

As extractivism started to deepen, legislators decided to bypass a series of environmental and social laws. Corporations were also advocating for the arrival of a new compassionate entrepreneur and, therefore, ready to embrace social corporate responsibility (CSR) values (I). Difficulties arise, however, when projects are active and operations start, generating a dilemma for policymakers: proceed with enforcing, or preserve the firms' rentability. Many analysts now argue that the soft approach has not been successful, with the empirical research demonstrating instead, weak regulatory enforcement and hands-down firm's misbehavior. Consider the case of

Pluspetrol oil operations in the Peruvian Amazon, as well as the State's inconsistent behavior.

In the 1990s, the Peruvian government decided to protect the indigenous peoples living in the Kugapakori-Nahua-Nanti Reserve.[8] Paradoxically, at the same time, national authorities were granting new gas concessions in lot 88 (75 percent of which overlaps with indigenous reserves). Pluspetrol environmental damages lead to IDLADS, a Lima-based institute, to initiate a series of lawsuits against the company – whose directives denied any wrongdoing. Despite their statements and CSR declarations, the company maintained a hands-off stance and even dishonored their environmental assessment duties[9]. Fortunately, the region also hosts other firms whose vision goes hand-in-hand with a stakeholder vision. Observe the case of a group of firms operating in Ecuador Northern Amazonia that decided to negotiate with local communities and offer some benefits to them.[10] The inclusion of a broader set of participants, though, continues to leaves away the effects of natural capital depletion either to count for its environmental impacts. Indirect stakeholders, therefore, might be deeply affected if the investment (for example) increases climate change risks. A tiny, but increasing number of countries and companies alike are trying to work for the common good. Cooperatives are an example of such organizational entities whose primary mission is to serve the community (S) in a sustainable way (E).

---

[8] Further protection was introduced in 2003, when the government enacted a Supreme Decree "guaranteeing [its] territorial integrity," banning "human settlements" different to those of the reserve's inhabitants, banning the "granting of new rights involving the exploitation of natural resources," and ensuring that "existing rights to exploit natural resources must be carried out with the maximum considerations to guarantee that the rights of the reserve's inhabitants are not affected," The Guardian, "Two lawsuits to stop Peru's most significant gas project in indigenous reserve." February 25, 2014.

[9] "Pluspetrol intenta declarar al OEFA incompetente en derrames de petróleo," www.servindi.org /actualidad-noticias/19/10/2016/pluspetrol-y-su-intento-por-declarar-incompetente-al-oefa-en-derrames.

[10] Oil firms decided to finance public works (road construction, waste handling, etc.), and to reduce environmental impacts (Bozigar et al., 2016).

Table 1 Framework for sustainable finance, with cases from Latin America

Value created	Ranking of factors	Optimization	Horizon	Example / Experiences	Industry	Type of firm	Government
Shareholder value	F	Max F	Short term	TEXACO Oriente - Ecuador	Nonrenewable Industry	Traditional	No regulation
Refined Shareholder value	F > S and E	Max F subject to S and E	Short term	TECPETROL Camisea - Peru	Nonrenewable Industry	Traditional	Soft regulation, weak enforcement
Stakeholder value	I = F + S + E	Optimize I	Medium term	Northern Ecuador Amazonia	Nonrenewable Industry	Corporate Social Responsible firm	Increasing regulation, increasing enforcement
Common good value	S and E > F	Optimize S and E subject to F	Long term	Costa Rica / Uruguay	Renewable Industry	Private firms/ Cooperatives / Public firms	Hard regulation & enforcement / Prohibition

Source: own elaboration after Schoenmaker and Schramade (2019)

Several authors (Lo, 2017; Thomä and Chenet, 2017; Chenet et al., 2019; Krogstrup and Oman, 2019) question the usefulness of such an approach. Markets are far from perfect; neither should investors be considered infallible. Moreover, the future is unknowable and unpredictable, which leads to a situation of radical uncertainty.[11]

Traditional risk management models do not reflect climate risks appropriately, as non-linear, non-cyclical, long-term risks are likely to be missed. A much more systematic approach should be taken for those trying to model climate change, accounting for the unpredictable, "green swans" events (Weitzman, 2009 and 2011; Kunreuther et al., 2012; Thomä and Chenet, 2017; Chenet et al., 2019; Bolton et al., 2020).[12] As a result of deep uncertainty, the use of backward-looking events to project the likelihood of future scenarios is inappropriate (Andersson et al., 2016; Tragedy of the Horizon, 2017). If an unexpected effect puts the society at risk, the government should frame its decisions to maintain the precautionary principle (PP) (Taleb et al., 2014). This principle is entitled "to deal with the effect of an absence of evidence and the incompleteness of scientific knowledge in some risky domains" (Taleb et al., 2014, p. 1), becoming of utmost importance in the context of climate change. A consequence of this global warming qualifies as a systematic "ruin" event, with adverse outcomes extending all scheduled times and having unlimited costs. All these flaws illustrate an epistemological breakpoint that calls for new, forward-looking alternatives (Zenghelis and Stern, 2016; Bolton et al., 2020).

The "tragedy of the horizon" imposes complex decisions while bringing new questions to the profession. How to transform the economic agents' decision-making process? How to mobilize funds to finance alternative energy if investments in traditional industries are more profitable than green ones? How does the presence of (market) failures and the (underdeveloped) nature of financial markets influence the outcome?

It implies leaving the short-term situation that currently characterizes the markets, which disregards the long-term risks and thus refrains from financing the infrastructure necessary to avoid such tragedy (Tragedy of the Horizon Program, 2017). Following Mark Carney's description of climate-related financial risks (CRFR), the Financial Stability Board (FSB) began to push for greater transparency, starting with the establishment of the industry-based Task Force on Climate-Related Financial Disclosure (TCFD).[13]

---

[11] Uncertainty could be further differentiated according its complexity and multiplicity, when dealing with climate change involves a combination of the two (Chenet et al., 2019).

[12] Therefore, inhibiting the use of the so-called Value at Risk (VaR) evaluation model.

[13] Disclosure and transparency are central to Pillar 3 of the International Basel regulatory framework, enacted after the global financial crisis.

The objective of this initiative is to spread the risks presented by the oil and gas industry and display all the investment opportunities presented by green markets. In other words, disclosure and transparency of information make investors aware of climate risks, and, therefore, make the funds move from carbon-intensive to clean energy sources. According to the initiative, if agents have information, they will act rationally and market discipline would be restated. This parallels to adapt the efficient market hypothesis to the "green" context (Christophers, 2017; Ameli et al., 2019; Chenet et al., 2019). For those working on behavioral economics and adaptative finance, the attitude of economic agents may be responding to habits, prior beliefs, or routines, all of which block optimal decision-making (Masini and Menichetti, 2012; Lo, 2017; Thomä and Chenet, 2017). Those who adopt the traditional, market-based vision consider that the funds (for green projects) will come as greater transparency (i.e., information) is given to investors. Another group of scholars highlights the public sector's role in the push, whether the push comes from public purchases or public banks (Mazzucato, 2015; Mazzucato and Semieniuk, 2018). Whereas some approaches might be more important than others, it is undoubtedly the work in all three domains that will make it possible to move forward with the transition to a green energy matrix.

While a new theory still must emerge, the use of old theoretical frameworks continues to misallocate the scarce funds arriving in the region. Whether all the highlighted shortcomings are being considered by oil and gas companies or not, undoubtedly, they should also be included by national oil companies (NOCs) in their decision process. Unfortunately, the rush for new reserves leads NOCs to look for new partners, to go behind new funding (bonds, equity). Whatever the political bent of the government in office, the race to increase reserves remains in force. The region could offer investors incentives and opportunities. However, when the project's financial viability correlates with high oil prices, problems are just around the corner: the probability that the assets will devalue keeps increasing. The search for short-term results continues to drive the energy investment logic of all companies, including NOCs. Alas, the attitude shows the disinterest of regional (and particularly, NOCs) oil and gas companies in climate change, not understanding that the peak demand is the real challenge to confront. Companies do not price the fossil fuel risk premium (Christophers, 2017),[14] which demonstrates market players' irrationality.

Some players, however, are starting to be worried about becoming lodged in a carbon bubble. Institutional investors also realize the importance of climate change–related risks, and how these affect their long-term returns. Opposition

---

[14] Premiums appear as projects do not adequately model the risks associates with climate-related regulation.

to traditional, nonrenewable energies is also mounting and not just in the streets but at large investors' board rooms. The other side of the coin is shown by the greater relevance of renewables and by market capitalization. Electric carmaker Tesla's market value has recently beat the US$ 100 billion milestone, surpassing the traditional VW, the world's second-largest carmaker (producing 30 million more cars than Tesla).

2.2 Investments in Nonrenewable Energy Resource

2.2.1 Investments and the Stranded Assets Problem

Climate change exposes investors to massive losses and to a new type of (physical) risk. A rapid transition, however, induces the likelihood of a (financial) risk. Physical and transition risks are strictly interconnected, although generating diametrically opposite effects. Henceforth, policy-makers are confronted with a decisional trade-off: a rapid phasing out of brown (or carbon-intensive) capital to minimize physical risks might heighten the transitional risk, while a delayed transition would reduce the financial fallout but expand real risks likelihood (Campiglio et al., 2018; Chenet et al., 2019; Bolton et al., 2020).

Transitional risks relate to the presence of the problem of stranded assets, reflecting a change in asset valuation. The University of Oxford's Stranded Assets Programme defines stranded assets as "assets that have suffered from unanticipated or premature write-downs, devaluations, or conversion to liabilities". In the specialized literature, the problem is said to relate to three different reasons: environmental, economic, or institutional (Caldecott et al., 2013; Caldecott, 2017). Alteration in value associated with environmental reasons, as climate events (floods, forest fires, tornadoes) could induce the government to advance with mitigation actions.

Economic factors could also be behind the stranded assets problem, as a sudden fall in the price of fossil fuel renders exploitation unprofitable. The fall would primarily affect those exhibiting higher costs or a high breakeven price. The continuous advances in renewable energy (RE) technologies accentuate the tumble (IRENA, 2014; Lilliestam, 2017), accelerating the diffusion of new technologies.[15] What can be seen in Figures 1.a, 1.b, and 1.c, and for all technologies graphed (onshore wind, solar PV, offshore wind, CSP), is the rapid decrease in installed and levelized costs, coupled with a simultaneous increase in capacity.

---

[15] Offshore turbines development might become a game changer, as their lower cost can transform the electricity market in the coming years. "Windpower has the capacity to meet the world's electricity demands," FT, 2019, www.ft.com/content/7c36dd38-f69b-11e9-a79c-bc9acae3b654.

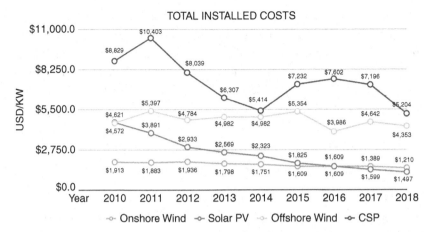

Figure 1.a Total installed costs, selected technologies (2010–18)

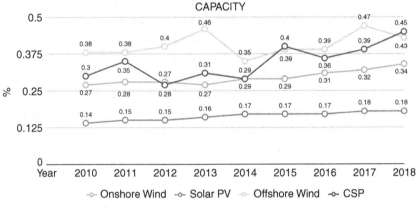

Figure 1.b Capacity, selected technologies (2010–18)

Prices for battery systems also continue to slip, and equipment is bringing higher storage capacity, causing fossil fuel demand to fall.[16] Advances in the automotive sector also count here, as the most disruptive technologies originate among electric-vehicle producers. Technological advances, therefore, continue transforming power generation and automotive markets.

A third factor affecting the market asset price relates to institutions (norms, laws, regulations), the emergence of a new environmental law, or a corollary of the enactment of a new regulation reducing the asset value. Institutional changes could originate abroad, beyond the influence of the

[16] The International Renewable Energy Agency estimates a 50–60 percent reduction by the year 2030 (IRENA, 2017).

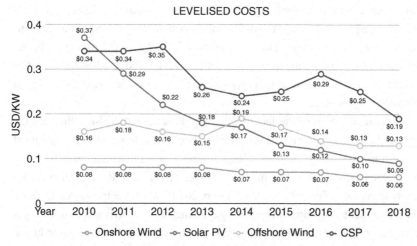

Figure 1.c Levelised costs, selected technologies (2010–18)
Source: IRENA, 2019a

fossil fuel producer. For example, some European cities are thinking of imposing a ban and ending fossil-fueled vehicle sales after 2025. Another example is the restrictions imposed on the use of diesel vehicles, as a response from local authorities to the rise of premature deaths from exposure to pollution[17]. Alternatively, the importer country could opt for imposing a border tax on carbon (Stiglitz, 2006; McKibbin et al., 2008). A similar option is under discussion at the European Union, where a broad and robust campaign against fossil fuels makes its implementation likely in the near future (Mehling et al., 2019).[18] Likewise, a proposal comes from Nobel Prize winner William Nordhaus (2020), whose plan to reduce emissions on global scale lies with the formation of a carbon club. Those who agree to participate should agree to reduce emissions through, for instance, fixing a minimum domestic carbon price. The club penalizes non-members and their exports are subject to a border tax.

The price reduction may also respond to a change in consumer attitudes (if choosing new, renewable energies), either "generated" from company decisions

---

[17] This is the experience of three Italian cities (Rome, Milan, and Turin), whose authorities are aiming to reduce premature deaths from exposure to pollution. "Rome, Milan, and Turin restrict the diesel vehicles due to pollution." El País, January 15, 2020.

[18] "Explainer: What an EU carbon border tax might look like and who would be hit," Reuters. December 10, 2019, www.reuters.com/article/us-climate-change-eu-carbontax-explainer/ explainer-what-an-eu-carbon-border-tax-might-look-like-and-who-would-be-hit-idUSKBN1YE1C4. "EU's carbon border tax plan is risky but needed," FT, www.ft.com/content/ 28bbb54c-41b5-11ea-a047-eae9bd51ceba.

decisions (opting for supplying from clean energy sources). Interest in traditional energy assets may dwindle, and investors may discontinue carbon-related project financing. The emergence of this "green" attitude adds the appearance of new financial instruments (as green bonds), whose availability accelerates the transition and, in this way, market innovation induces the fall in traditional asset value.

Additionally, each of the factors affecting the asset value also influences the financial risk associated with a particular technology, in terms of its development and diffusion. Whereas in the past, higher outlay costs prevented the diffusion of new, green technologies, this might no longer be the case: RE capital costs are lower than those of the oil industry (Nelson, 2018). Whatever the source, in short, the divestment decision will end up generating a grave crisis for oil and gas companies. The crisis will also have vast repercussions on the banking industry, given its exposure to the oil sector (Battiston et al., 2016).

The government should carefully observe NOCs' indebtedness policy, as their debts might finally be accounted for as public (Manley et al., 2017 and 2019). Not only does excessive indebtedness generate risks, but climate change might also put the companies in jeopardy. NOCs, in short, appear less prepared to face the challenges posed by the transition (Cust et al., 2017),[19] which policymakers should consider when planning the medium-to-long term. this might end up affecting public budgets and generating a problem of "stranded nations."

Globally, the oil industry maintains assets for US $25 trillion, adding US $1 trillion per year (IRENA, 2019b, p. 84) – an investment flow incompatible with what was agreed in Paris, 2015. Therein lies the climate–financial risk: additional investments that will not be repaid transform into worthless assets (Carbon Tracker Initiative, 2019a and 2020b)[20]. Table 2 lists a series of oil projects, particularly the largest launched by Latin American governments in recent years (2018–19) (Mexico and Brazil), whose continuation implies going beyond sustainability development goals. What stands out in the table is the continual search for new projects, despite the NDB commitments.

Several empirical studies show that non-traditional fuel projects have a high breakeven price (BEP), expanding the stranded asset problem[21]. However, the oil industry continues to obtain resources that entail risks. Even so, neither

---

[19] "State oil companies underprepared for transition to cleaner fuels," FT. January 19, 2020.

[20] Stranded asset loses might be US$ 1–4 trillion (Mercure et al., 2018, Carbon Tracker Initiative, 2018a).

[21] The breakeven price is the business unit value required to generate earnings before interest, taxes, depreciation/depletion, amortization, and exploration (EBITDAX) equal to maintenance capital expenditures plus interest. In other words: Breakeven Price: $P + E + OWD + T + A\&S$ [P: production costs, E: exploring costs, OWD: oil well development costs, T: Transportation costs, and A&S: administrative and selling costs].

Table 2 The stranded assets threat: Latin America's largest projects sanctioned in 2018 & 2019 outside the SDS budget

Asset	Country	2019–2030 capex ($bn)	Resource theme	Partners (* denotes operator	Status	Year of announcement
Amoca FFD, MX	Mexico	1.4	Conventional (land/shelf)	Eni*, Qatar Petroleum		2018
Mizton FFD, MX	Mexico	0.7	Conventional (land/shelf)	Eni*, Qatar Petroleum		2018
Jubarte (pre-salt) (Parque das Baleia FPSO), BR	Brazil	4.3	Deep water	Petrobras*	Approval expected 2019	2019
Buzios (x-Franco) V, BR	Brazil	3.9	Ultra deep water	Petrobras*	Approval expected 2019	2019
Mero 2 (x-Libra NW), BR	Brazil	3.7	Ultra deep water	Petrobras*, Shell, CNPC (parent), Total, CNOOC	Approved June 2019	2019
Lapa (x-Carioca) Southwest (BM-S-9), BR	Brazil	1.2	Ultra deep water	Total*, Shell, Repsol, Sinpec Group (parent)	Unclear	2019
Neon/Neon Sul (x-Echidna), BR	Brazil	0.8	Deep water	Karoon Energy*	Development plan due Q3 2019	2019

Source: Carbon Tracker Initiative

policymakers nor local business groups have sized risks, nor have the financial system has done so (Caldecott et al., 2016).

Notably, the stock of stranded assets is directly related to the value adopted by the ton of carbon and the level of renewable energy subsidies, both policies beyond (Latin American) oil-exporting countries. Recent research by Frederick van der Ploeg and Armon Rezai (2018) has demonstrated that the (stranded asset) problem aggravates as the closer we get to the peak warming target, the higher the climate sensitivity for cumulative emissions and the cheaper production through renewable energy. Remarkably, all three conditions are now approaching.

As a significant producer of coal, the problem of stranded assets for Colombia is acute. To keep global temperatures below 2 °C, 80 percent of coal reserves should remain unused (McGlade and Etkins, 2015), add 720 GW reduction in capacity by 2030 (36 percent) (Cui et al., 2019). Fortunately, the coal industry confronts a gloomy financial present and no future (Buckley, 2019). When comparing LCOE terms, coal generation is now above renewables (Carbon Tracker Initiative, 2018b). Colombian authorities, in sum, should think twice and reconsider investing in new coal projects, but also in the construction of new coal power utilities.[22] The government could reduce the stranded asset risk and redirect current subsidies to fund renewables (Strambo et al., 2018).

Utilities might also confront a stranded asset problem, particularly if regulators (for whatever reason) decide to accelerate fossil fuel power plant lifetimes before firms' investment repayment period.[23] Henceforth, energy planners should consider this when assessing the impact of utility infrastructure investment projects. In other words, regulators should evaluate the committed carbon emissions associated with both existing infrastructure (Davies and Socolow, 2014) and planned projects (Edenhofer et al., 2018, Pfeiffer et al., 2018)[24]. If to date renewable sources (basically, hydroelectric sources) have had a crucial role in Latin American power generation, most of the recent incremental additions are associated with the construction of (mainly gas but also carbon) nonrenewable power stations. Additionally, new gas pipelines are under construction, with eighty years of technical life (for gas-fired power plant, up to forty years). In consideration of the goal of net-zero CO_2 emissions by 2050, all these projects should be re-evaluated. A recent Inter-

---

[22] The capital recovery period for coal power plants used to be forty or more years, although new projects are calculating a lower repayment period between thirty-five and twenty years to meet the 2.0 °C and 1.5 °C scenario respectively (Cui et al., 2019; Carbon Tracer Initiative, 2020b).

[23] According to Davis and Socolow (2014), the lifetime of power generation for different technological sources (in years): coal (37), natural gas (35), and oil (32).

[24] CarbonBriefs maps global coal power (see www.carbonbrief.org/mapped-worlds-coal-power-plants).

American Bank report highlights how all these projects came to challenge the non-proliferation (NDB) commitments, henceforth, affecting their proposed budgets. If countries go ahead with their investment plans "utilities in the region would need to close prematurely 10 percent to 16 percent of the existing fossil fueled capacity, respectively, or reduce the utilization rate of existing plants to the same effect" to keep in line with their commitments (González-Mahecha et al., 2019). To sum up, sooner than later, the stranded asset problem would critically affect utilities.

2.2.2 Investments and Technological Lock-In

If investments are reversible, then, the stranded asset is not a problem (Ploeg and Rezai, 2018). It is the irreversible character of the investment that matters,[25] which reinforces the use of a particular carbon-intensive technology. This characteristic is associated with the concept of a dependent path that relates to the persistence of past events and how it prevents (or delays) the adoption of renewable energies (Erickson et al., 2015; Seto et al., 2016). The technological decision might, then, lead to an unsustainable lock-in (Loorbach et al., 2017). For example, the decision to invest in a new combined cycle power plant: the lock-in inversely associates with the marginal production costs.

From a climate change perspective, the lock-in potential directly associates with the equipment's life horizon. It denotes the scale to the accumulated emissions generated by the project. Besides the capital asset amortization link, Erickson et al. (2015) consider the financial barrier imposed by the lock-in (measured concerning the value of carbon). This barrier generates an extra cost of capital, new funds necessary to replace the "polluting" equipment ahead of time.

According to the literature, the persistence of the path responds to factors beyond the company domain or will, including workers' decisions preventing the change. Lock-in can also respond to cultural (consumption habits) or political (the presence of specific policies or institutions) factors (Unruh, 2000; Foxon, 2002; Seto et al., 2016). Nor can the carbon lobby (renewable energy) be ignored (Fouquet, 2016). Whatever the origin, the phenomenon increases the exit as well as the financial costs associated with the replacement (Erikson et al., 2015; Seto et al., 2016).

The scale of the project determines the severity of the problem: the larger the investment, the harder it becomes to get out of it. Similar reasoning applies at the national level. Take the unconventional fossil deposit of Vaca Muerta – Neuquén basin, in whose development the Argentinean government is sinking

---

[25] This relates to the "sunk investment" concept use by the Industrial Organization literature.

substantial amounts of funds.[26] Once the capital is sunk, any attempt to end the production would become prohibitive. Add all the funds are going to infrastructure (gas pipelines, ports for the dispatch of liquefied natural gas, refinery capacity), which would remain unaffected if external markets shut down. The development is taking considerable capital expenses, whose subsequent repayment period extends in time. Vaca Muerta, henceforth, might expose Argentina to greater financial exposure.

2.3 Energy Matrix Transformation: Investing and Citizens' Participation

When addressing the transition, policymakers should take both operative and capital costs into account. Although equipment prices have been experiencing a downward trend, the presence of substantial initial outlay costs continues to impose obstacles for RE dissemination (IPCC, 2012; Waissbein et al., 2013; Ondraczek et al., 2015; Hirth and Steckel, 2016; Best, 2017; Best and Burke, 2018; Halstead et al., 2018).

Consider the case of photovoltaic solar panels (PVs). For geographical reasons, many Latin American countries might opt for an expansion as solar radiation guarantees highly competitive production prices for electricity. Despite low operating expenses and (practically null) marginal costs, initial capital expenditures remain substantial. This imposes an extensive repayment period. In the presence of perfect markets and low-interest rates, new solar parks could fund at low costs. International financial markets, however, are rather imperfect. Therefore, and even when marginal costs are significantly lower in (for instance) Guatemala than in Germany, are the financial costs (commonly referred to as WACC[27]) that disables the former to install the new, cleaner technology. When deciding investments, therefore, WACC differentials might be more important than the variation in radiation in terms of different location impacts on marginal costs.

The financial project should also consider the price at which the tonne of carbon is valued in the country, as energy prices reflect both taxes and subsidies. Both concepts are necessary to understand why PVs are installed in Denmark but no through Ecuador. Fossil fuel subsidies give brown producers an additional

---

[26] The Neuquén basin in Northern Patagonia (provinces of Neuquén, Río Negro, Mendoza, and La Pampa). Dubbed "Vaca Muerta" ("Dead Cow"), it has been identified as the biggest shale play outside North America and makes Argentina the third country, after the United States and Canada, to reach commercial development ["Vaca Muerta Megaproject: A Fracking Carbon Bomb in Patagonia," Enlace por la Justicia Energética y Socioambiental (EJES), 2017]

[27] The weighted average cost of capital (WACC) is a calculation of a firm's cost of capital in which each category of capital is proportionately weighted. All sources of capital, including common stock, preferred stock, bonds, and any other long-term debt, are included in a WACC calculation.

advantage, preventing "green challengers" from entering into the Ecuadorian energy market (Schmidt et al., 2012; Whitley, 2013; Zahno and Castro, 2017).

All of these costs boil down to a single, comparative measure: the levelized cost of energy (LCOE), comprising capital costs and long-run marginal costs, the later including the costs of the particular fuel used for electricity production and (variable and fixed) costs.

LCOE: capital costs + LRMC

LCOE can be roughly calculated as the net present value of all costs over the lifetime of the asset divided by an appropriately discounted total of the energy output from the asset (currency per kilowatt-hour or megawatt-day) over that lifetime (an average, twenty to forty years). Once obtained, it should be determined whether the consumer will be able to pay the incremental fee required by the new, renewable equipment. Therefore, and despite a larger WACC, as LCOE keeps diminishing, green projects are now becoming feasible almost everywhere.

So far, the cost of capital faced by renewables was above that paid by oil companies. Recently, the relationship reversed as the market has begun to discount climate–financial risk (the stranded asset effect starts to affect oil companies). Therefore, incumbent benefits begin to evaporate: belonging no longer generates privileges but becomes a burden. This should alert producer countries and induce state enterprises (NOCs) to move faster with their investments in renewables.

Latin America is beginning the process of transforming its energy matrix, with many countries advancing the installation of renewable sources (see Table 3). The Uruguay case is worthy of note, particularly for the speed with which authorities have transformed the energy matrix (Gramkow et al., 2020). Other countries have emulated it, making remarkable progress in the generation mix.

The presence of market failures justifies the introduction of mechanisms that encourage the emergence of renewable energy technologies (RETs), thus favoring the replacement of polluting sources. This is because the price of electricity generation does not adequately reflect its costs. In other words, in order to guarantee "clean" production, the state pays the incremental cost faced by those who are willing to enter the market.[28]

Several Latin American countries are beginning to compromise with renewable, fixing targets and attracting funds. Public auctions have become one of the

---

[28] "Incremental cost" means the difference between the cost of conventional and renewable electricity.

Table 3 Renewable energy, all sources, select countries

	Capacity (MW)			Production (GWh)		
	2010	2018	(%)	2010	2017	(%)
World	1,223,355	2,536,346	107.3%	4,199,274	6,190,948	47.43%
Argentina	9,649	11,935	23.7%	34,513	42,224	22.34%
Bolivia	584	905	55.0%	2,288	2,423	5.90%
Brazil	89,558	135,674	51.5%	437,013	465,568	6.53%
Chile	6,158	10,903	77.1%	24,298	34,979	43.96%
Colombia	9,457	12,319	30.3%	41,957	59,314	41.37%
Costa Rica	1,889	3,070	62.5%	8,871	11,214	26.41%
Ecuador	2,345	5,164	120.2%	8,875	20,685	133.07%
El Salvador	785	1,289	64.2%	3,892	4,169	7.12%
Guatemala	1,311	2,995	128.5%	4,919	8,041	63.47%
Honduras	620	1,660	167.7%	3,235	5,439	68.13%
Mexico	13,515	22,128	63.7%	45,747	51,501	12.58%
Nicaragua	381	690	81.1%	1,358	2,555	88.14%
Panama	957	2,261	136.3%	4,220	7,945	88.27%
Paraguay	8,810	8,849	0.4%	54,065	59,694	10.41%
Peru	3,516	6,252	77.8%	20,286	30,810	51.88%
Uruguay	1,815	3,728	105.4%	9,586	14,114	47.24%
Venezuela	14,626	15,192	3.9%	76,779	55,830	−27.28%

Source: own elaboration after data from IRENA (2019)

most widely adopted schemes (Lewis, 2011; IRENA, 2013; Kuntze and Moerenhout, 2013; Hansen et al., 2019; Viscidi and Yepez, 2020), with the region playing a leading role in it (GEF, 2017). In order to spread "clean," however, other mechanisms were introduced (for example, such as granting tax incentives or setting a portfolio of renewables in the production mix).[29] The auction, however, generally favors large-scale projects (Böckler and Giannini Pereira, 2018).

In order to achieve energy justice, however, schemes like the feed-in tariffs (FIT) are more helpful (Jacobs et al., 2013). FIT guarantees facilitated repayment of RES installation loans, as it resembles a long-term provision contract (commonly, a period of fifteen to twenty years).[30] In addition to guaranteeing prices (rate) and quantities (supply), contracts often stipulate access to the interconnection network (Couture and Ganon, 2010; Jacobs and Sovacool, 2012). Briefly, the FIT scheme differentiates rates, among other aspects, by contract length, plant size, source, purchase options, and location. Differences could also be responding to the rate structure: fixed price (payment delinked from markets) or premium price (payments aligns with the market).[31] Anyway, FIT alone does not guarantee goal achievement, as the case of Spain illustrates.[32]

RETs allow for a smaller scale, lowering initial capital needs. Projects could adopt a decentralized structure, bringing new opportunities for participation and community involvement. The other side of the coin, though, is the higher transaction costs (while presenting a lower rate of return). This opens the door to cooperatives, an organizational form widely adopted in the German energy transition (Energiewende), and particularly active in disseminating the use of solar PV sources (Yildiz, 2014; Yildiz et al., 2015; Lofwitzsch, 2018a).

Considering the shortcomings presented by the traditional finance framework (see Section 2.1), then renewable energy cooperatives (RE co-ops) qualify as a better option (Yildiz, 2014; Yildiz et al., 2015; Mignon and Rüdinger, 2016;

---

[29] The tax exception scheme offers different types of incentives, which may be granted at the time of production, investment, or consumption. The RPS mechanism, on the other hand, obliges utilities to generate a certain percentage of their production from renewables, for which they receive a certificate (the so-called green transferable certificate).

[30] It recognizes generation costs plus a prize, but on a (decreasing) scale to stimulate technological innovation.

[31] Fixed schemes present lower risks than those based on a prize, whereas the latter tends to ensure investment at a lower cost. Some jurisdictions opt for a tariff mix (as does Spain), which allows investors to choose the system by which they prefer to be remunerated. Henceforth, differentiating producers according to the level of risk he wishes to assume

[32] The Spanish government instituted a very ambitious PV plan, promising favorable tariffs to participant firms. Years later, however, authorities decided on significant retrospective cuts on remuneration for solar PV, wind, and concentrated solar power (CSP) (RES, 2013).

Lo, 2017; Holstenkamp, 2018; Lofwitzsch, 2018a; Rajan, 2019; Schoenmaker and Schramade, 2019). RE co-ops do not pursue profit maximization but attempt to bring benefits to their associates (as the provision of services) (behavioral economics). RE co-ops consider consumers as heterogeneous, all having limited information (bounded rationality), and with members responding to fairness instead of utilitarian behavior. RE co-ops are (basically) funded by equity, with (patient capital) members' natural predisposition being for long-term financing projects. RE co-ops' predilection for solar PV associates with the scale and for the simplicity of its technology, which easily permits consumers to become producers (prosumers). Duality induces incentive complementarity, therefore complementing flexibility in consumption (demand) with greater energy efficiency (supply) (Lowitzsch, 2018b).

In addition to sharing needs (energy) and political ideals and social preferences (new sources, non-polluting), proximity dramatically influences the success of community energy players as cooperatives.[33] For this to happen, it is essential to envision the transition from a political economy perspective, to observe the interests of all involved actors at the time of designing (Böckler and Giannini Pereira, 2018; Feron et al., 2018).[34] Policymakers should critically review the present regulatory framework if, for instance, their objective is to install new categories of actors (i.e., individual or collective prosumers).[35] They should also move away from the ideal electricity market; the "one-size-fits-all" paradigm often replicates in the design of public auctions. RE tenders' rules should be adopted to allow and incentivize different forms of community participation.[36] This means, when possible, getting behind small-scale projects (MW not GW).

Up-front investments are financially fixed under a FIT scheme, employing a long-term electricity sales contract among cooperative members.[37] Funds could also originate from real estate tax deductions, the establishment of a special VAT regime, or by guaranteeing a minimum price (for electricity being sold), and net-metering (allowing injection of surplus production accumulating energy

---

[33] Communitary energy (CEs) providers should be thought of as a broader category, encompassing community trusts, non-profit organisations, charities, and RE co-ops.

[34] Power utilities and concessionaires could be reluctant to expand net metering systems, or to pay a fair tariff to prosumers feeding the grid.

[35] When becoming prosumers, residential consumers assume a positive behavioral change in energy consumption.

[36] Cooperatives have long been involved in the energy sector through different activities (generation, distribution, services), playing an important role in electricity market diffusion in Latin America.

[37] The popularity of the FIT scheme for cooperatives originates in Germany, but the device was also installed by other countries, including the UK; Denmark; Ontario, Canada (Tarhan, 2015); and Brazil (Böckler and Giannini Pereira, 2018).

credits).[38] Private actors (energy companies, integrators, installers of PV systems) could finance households (whose repayment originates in energy savings). Governments could also institute some financial facilities, grants, or preferential loans to benefit those living in the most impoverished neighbors or shantytowns. The legal framework could also recognize the figure of "energy community," and to incentivize its financial participation via equity in a RE installation. Some rural communities could also co-manage local facilities (for example, small-scale wind projects, biomass plants, or small hydropower) and develope a local grid, perhaps with a point of connection to the national grid.

Countries should set bright and ambitious targets for decentralized RE production to advance with the transition. When designing the scheme, policy-makers should, in particular, make room for collective, community participation if they aim to eliminate energy poverty. They should also address financial, technological, and organizational barriers, but, above all, policymakers should "help communities develop new business models, as well as affordable and accessible demand-side management schemes" (Campos et al., 2020). Policymakers, however, should take cultural and local circumstances into account when planning the ER diffusion. Those having a short time horizon concerning their investment decisions make these technologies unappealing, and a cultural barrier widely disseminates in the region as described by Feron et al. (2018) for the case of Chile.

3 Climate Change, Energy Transition, and Social Inclusion

The productive model prevailing in Latin American plays a critical role in the high levels of inequalities prevailing in our societies – a persevering structural characteristic resisting boom-and-bust cycles (ECLAC, 2016). The good, the bad, and the ugly: all types of governments have profited from natural resource exploitation, a policy matrix patchwork that led the region to social stratification, residential segregation, and conflicts. Unfortunately, climate change raises new challenges for policymakers: an inter-generational dilemma with skewed vulnerabilities, at both local and global levels. These dilemmas are directly interconnected to the underlying development model, which further complicates the phasing out of fossil fuels (basically associated with the imposition of a carbon tax and the removing subsidies). This chapter attempts to show why fixing the climate change problem raises new political disputes, at both local and international levels.

---

[38] In Brazil, the coverage was extended to condominiums, consortiums, cooperatives, and remote self-consumption.

If the opposing poles of conflict and consensus accompany modern democracies (Schumpeter, 1942; Przeworski, 2010; Ragazzoni, 2018), the involvement of civil society actors (participation) is currently perceived as enriching it (Habermas, 1981; Vitale, 2006; Newig and Kvarda, 2012). Thus far, it becomes key to evaluate how the different political schemes articulate citizen participation, and thus legitimizes the ET process. Central to the analysis is the concept of the fair and just energy transition, to tackle climate change and create prosperity simultaneously (McCauley and Heffron, 2018).[39]

The purpose of this section is to assess the effects all these distributional factors have on the transition dynamics. However, the traditional, technical approach to the decision-making process often disregards the distributional dimension. This prevents the irruption of a smooth transition path, but disrupts social conflict. The challenges are even more compelling globally, particularly for oil-exporting countries, as the transition might severely affect their exports (and fiscal earnings). The lack of coordination between producing countries, added to the finite nature of the oil resources, certainly does not help in finding a cooperative solution.

3.1 Democracy, Public Goods and Citizen Participation

The mid 1980s marked the region's return to democracy, a comeback coinciding with the ISI model's decline (the balance of payments constraint was its Achilles' heel). Forced to opt for a new economic model, Latin America decided to embark on a process of economic liberalization and openness. A natural resource, export-led model, was restored. Mass democracy was back, but redistribution policies proved challenging to sustain. The new macro-economic configuration permitted elites to arbitrate and place their savings in some tax-free haven in the face of any attempt to reduce inequality (Solimano, 2012; Solimano, 2015; Pond, 2017). Latin American democratic return showed highly unstable equilibria from its very beginning, challenging economic development and social cohesion.

The democratic return also coincides with greater legal recognition for Latin American historically forgotten minorities: indigenous peoples. For most governments, recognizing indigenous people's rights became a policy priority in a region with more than 45 million people and more than 800 groups. Consequently, several countries decided to grant constitutional status to

---

[39] The just transition concept encapsulates three former, partial perspectives on the issue (climate justice, energy justice, and environmental justice (McCauley and Heffron, 2018).

Resolution 169 of the International Labor Organization (ILO) (1989).[40] From a political perspective, this recognition might assimilate to the establishment of a plain liberal democracy. Indigenous "free, prior, and informed consent" (voice) was a precondition for extractive firms' operation, putting participation in a central position. Not only were rights extended to native peoples, but governments also were keen to advance with the environmental agenda. This predisposition opened the door to the enactment of specific laws to introduce new regulations protecting the environment (Chancel and Piketty, 2015; Sonnenfeld and Taylor, 2018).

Furthermore, following the green spirit observed at the Rio Conference,[41] policymakers decided to implement participatory policy decision-making schemes. The idea of sustainable development in the UN 2030 Agenda for Sustainable Development identifies governance as a critical pillar, highlighting the relevance of people's participation, voice, and vote. Participation enhances the effectiveness of the decision-making process; it empowers citizens and legitimate democracy (Newig and Kvarda, 2012).

Driven by the rise of China, the pressure for natural resources led to exploitation of areas outside the scope of the market, like the Amazons, penetrating into isolated and pristine biodiverse ecosystems in indigenous territories (Finer et al., 2008; Ray et al., 2017). Unfortunately, this new search for a new "El Dorado" has left democratic values behind. Most of the time, the mandatory "free, prior, and informed consent" ended up as an empty slogan. Tough, legally empowered indigenous peoples continued to suffer from ethnic and racial discrimination (ECLAC, 2016). Living in poor and remote areas with (almost) no state presence, indigenous peoples also suffer from territorial discrimination. A similar treatment is received by shantytown settlers, slum populations, and segregated minorities, all widely exposed to waste, pollution, inadequate infrastructure, and lacking access to energy. All are liekwise neglected by authorities, configuring the second dimension of territorial discrimination. The contradiction reveals the limitations democracies have in Latin America: how certain circles of power

---

[40] Indigenous peoples' self determination would be recognized by the UN the United Nations Declaration on the Rights of Indigenous Peoples (2007), and a series of declarations including the Montevideo Consensus on Population and Development (2013).

[41] According to Article 22 of the Rio Declaration of 1992, "Environmental issues are best handled with the participation of all concerned citizens, at the relevant level. At the national level, each individual shall have appropriate access to information concerning the environment that is held by public authorities, including information on hazardous materials and activities in their communities, and the opportunity to participate in decision-making processes" 12 August 1992 A/CONF.151/26 (Vol. I) Report of the United Nations Conference on Environment and Development, www.un.org/en/development/desa/population/migration/gener alassembly/docs/globalcompact/A_CONF.151_26_Vol.I_Declaration.pdf.

persist in influencing the public agenda, blocking social rights, and watering down environmental regulations.

Democracy should guarantee all citizens (including minorities) to be considered in government decisions, particularly those directly affecting them. When the rights of some groups are left aside and not listened to in the decision-making process, democracy is said to have a non-liberal character (Zakaria, 1997). Mukand and Rodrik (2015) define liberal democracy as a "regime in which civil rights are provided in addition to electoral and property rights," and describe modeling civil rights as the nondiscriminatory provision of public goods (justice and free speech, education, wealth, and infrastructure): we add environmental goods to the list (Stanley, 2020).

The democratic–liberal agenda, which has expanded social and environmental rights since the late 1980s, however, came to collide with the extractive model. In this context, it is difficult to agree on long-term development policies that are socially inclusive and environmentally sustainable. A new type of inequality emerges in the design, between those whose voice is being considered and those who remain marginalized (and, often, the most exposed to environmental degradation) (ECLAC, 2014a; Chancel and Piketty, 2015; Davis and Diffenbaugh, 2016; Piketty, 2020). A non-liberal democracy, therefore, associates with the presence of a regime captured by commercial or clientelistic interests, which disregards the rights, perspectives, and interests of the minorities that inhabit the country (Smith and Sells, 2016). Power concentration, in brief, prevents Latin American governments from advancing towards a participatory and decentralized energy transition process (Mitchell, 2009; Noboa and Upham, 2018; LeQuesney, 2019).

The energy transition could be thought of as a new arena for political disputes. The resolution might reinforce the actual (concentrated) pattern of electricity generation and distribution, helping induce a more decentralized participative scheme. Technically, both are feasible. Unlike the current energy paradigm, renewables allow for greater geographic decentralization, a smaller scale of operation, a role for cooperatives, and the opportunity for consumers to become suppliers (prosumers) (IEA, 2017; Gallucci, 2019; Runney, 2019).[42] All these characteristics allow for greater participation. From an institutional, organizational-level perspective, social inclusion favors feed-in-tariffs schemes over auctions, opening the door to more democratic, cooperative structures (megawatts) instead of necessarily siding with large firms (gigawatts) (see Section 2.3). If the transition intents to get around the

---

[42] There is evidence of a significant drop in the cost of renewables (solar panels; wind) while advancing intelligent distribution systems that allow consumers to sell their surpluses. The number of pro-consumers is expected to rise to 75 billion in 2025.

social dimension, then it should look beyond efficiency and cost-effectiveness solutions (Finley-Brook and Holloman, 2016; McCauley and Heffron, 2018). Justice in transition implies respect for human rights. However, it also comprises recognition of local population voice and participation. Greater decentralization also brings resilience to the electricity grid, helping to overcome energy security concerns. Unfortunately, The voice of those who lay behind the poorest often remain silent. Rulers' attitude, in other words, arouses social conflict.[43] Participation is needed to empower the poorer and unprotected, and to bring liberal democracy back.

3.2 Public Policies: Global Problems, Local Responses

The climate mitigation toolbox considers carbon pricing as the first-best policy, whose most simple scheme consists of fixing a marginal rate that equals the damage generated by fuel use. The so-called Pigouvian tax simultaneously obtains economic efficiency while correcting for the externality (Stern, 2007). Authorities, then, calculate a shadow price for carbon, and that is it. Unfortunately, in the real world, things are more complicated. If inequality is excessive, and can not be corrected by direct transfers, then a single carbon tax is no longer socially optimal (Chichilniski and Heal 1994; Fleubaey et al., 2019).

As a global negative externality, though, climate change resolution is even more complicated: all benefit from the fighting, but each country wants to be a free-rider. However, and despite all shortcomings, the environmental tax kept expanding. Though, in most jurisdictions, carbon is not taxed, and "about three-quarters of the emissions that are covered by a carbon priced below US $10/tCO_2$" (Stiglitz and Stern, 2017). Henceforth, and in order to attain the objectives committed in Paris, a more significant fiscal effort is needed. A recent International Monetary Fund report evaluates setting the carbon tax at US$ 75/tC02 (IMF, 2019), whereas the High-Level Commission on Carbon Prices recommends a range of US$40–80/tCO_2 (Stiglitz and Stern, 2017).

3.2.1 The local response

The level of inequality (Piketty, 2014 and 2020; Boix, 2003; Solt 2008; Scheidel, 2017), and its multidimensional scope (Therborn 2012; ECLAC, 2016; Combet and Méjean, 2017), strongly influence modern democracies progress or decadence. The achievement of greater equality involves a better distribution of means (income, productive and financial assets, and property), as

---

[43] The Environmental Justice Atlas brings a visual explanation of the magnitude of the conflict in Latin America (www.envjustice.org).

well as capacities, autonomies, and reciprocal recognition and, fundamentally, to the enjoyment of equal rights (CEPAL, 2016 and 2019).

Previous studies have unanimous demonstrate that climate crisis particularly harms those living in the bottom, bringing inequality at the center stage mitigation policies. For policymakers, it involves thinking in the design, but also on: how the transition is being paid? Who wins, who loses?

The poorest usually spend the largest slide of their income on carbon-intensive goods, which places distributive issues at the forefront. It confronts the ruler to the trade-off between efficiency and equity (Newell and Mulaney, 2013; Rosenbloom, 2016; Pigott et al., 2019). On the one hand, the tax benefits the environment while inducing a reduction in greenhouse gases. On the other hand, it might adversely impact households' consumption expenditures as they increase the price of essential goods. A carbon tax might lead to an increase in the electricity bill, for instance, affecting all households[44]. Environmental taxes are mostly regressive, however, as consumption spending decrease with income levels. Those at the bottom quintile uses public transport more than those at the uppest, the affluent class. Inequality, therefore, might be perceived as political and arising from the implementation of environmental policies (Chancel and Piketty, 2015; Piketty, 2020). The challenge for the government, then, is to design a transition regime that provides the expected environmental benefits (disincentive fossil fuel use) well, at the same time, avoids to affect the most vulnerable sectors (Combet and Méjean, 2017; Klenert et al., 2018; Hsiang et al., 2018; Douenne, 2019; Vogt-Schilb et al., 2019). The proposed scheme should consider income levels, and differentiate households according to their quintile position: poor, middle income (second to the fourth quintile), and wealthier. Thus, if what tries to prioritize is equity, the policymaker could establish some sort of (indirect or direct) compensation benefiting those belonging to the most deprived groups[45]. In this sense, the solution would be to introduce a non-linear tax on labor (to redistribute)[46], and Pigouvian taxation (to reduce negative externalities) (Cremer et al., 1998 and 2003; Aigner, 2013; Jacobs and van der Ploeg, 2019)[47].

---

[44] The increase directly responds to the fossil fuel share in the electricity generation mix.

[45] Note that for an important group of Latin American countries, distribution by income quintile directly connects with people's ethnicity and race (ECLAC, 2016; page 28) – it also connects with territory.

[46] Revenues from the tax are use to reduce labor taxes (or in indirect taxes), hencerfoth, increasing workers' disposable income. Therefore, the social planner is attaining a double dividend: reducing C02 emmissions (first dividend) along an improvements in the labor markets (second dividend)

[47] According to the Atkinson – Stiglitz public finance theorem, all agents observe externality in the same way. Under such circumstances distributive considerations should be not consider. Otherwise, equity issues must be recognized by the social planner.

Developing countries might confront more challenges when trying to obtain this double dividend, as most of their population is in a situation of labor informality (Devarajan et al., 2011). Informality is a critical factor that prevents the establishment of (indirect) compensation schemes like those centered on labor. In order to keep the double dividend alive, governments could make use of social programs or cash transfer schemes (Vogt-Schilb et al., 2019; Schaffitzel et al., 2019). Besides all the flaws, it represents a direct way of redistributing wealth if the social planner has insufficient information on the most vulnerable households (Combet and Méjean, 2017). The IDB study evaluates a series of alternatives [to introduce a specific poverty rebate, to maintain (augment) the current-enrolees, or to introduce a universal rebate] to compensate those left behind (Vogt-Schilb et al., 2019)[48]. After that, it gauges a series of alternatives for funding the proposal, including now a perfect (although unfeasible) compensation scheme[49].

Direct and indirect schemes, then, permit to match efficiency with equity, bringing a "double dividend" to the economy[50]. Independently of which of them is finally being chosen, traditional tax models are assuming within-group homogeneity, permitting authorities to infer in which category a particular household locates and, accordingly, to relocate subsidies and funds.

Homogeneity, however, might be a rather exceptional event, not the rule. CO_2 emissions respond to multiple drivers, not just to income levels. Of utmost importance for policymakers, henceforth, is to understand the multidimensional nature of inequality. While traditionally, analysts have considered differences in use according to social groups (vertical differentiation), they exclude the possibility of observing asymmetries within the same social group (horizontal differentiation), which relates to other variables. For example, consider the residence location: a poor rural peasant from Peru needs to use its vehicle, whereas an urban poor living in a shantytown in Lima might profit from her proximity to the public transport system (if subsidized by the central government). Although belonging to the same category, tough, both individuals face a different level of (transport) expenses. From an economic perspective, this means that elasticities within the same grouping are not constant. If

---

[48] The IDB study, covering 16 Latin American countries, evaluates how the introduction of a $ 30 carbon tax affect different households (being differentiated in 5 quintiles). Among all suggested options, the poverty targeted rebate seems to be the more progressive in the cases of Argentina, Bolivia, Brazil, Chile, Honduras, Nicaragua, Panama, and Paraguay. Expanding the enrollment base becomes preferable for other countries: Colombia, Costa Rica, Ecuador, Guatemala, Mexico, Peru, and Uruguay.

[49] As it requires detailed knowledge of each households expenditure schemes.

[50] European countries in the 1990s were the first to introduce the DD scheme, aimed to shift taxation burden from labor (reducing) to energy (increasing). Some countries were also r redirecting funds out from subsidies to labor training.

heterogeneity is present at the group's interior, then the compensation might not reach those who need it the most. Ultimately, when assessing the distributional impact, the "type of tax, their design, the nature of the encumbered asset, and the specificities of the economies to which they apply" should be considered (Vera, 2019).

A similar, distributional analysis should be considered when governments intend to reduce or eliminate subsidies. From an economic perspective, the presence of subsidies always implies a distortion. They are aggravated here, as it encourages the use of polluting sources (fossil fuels) instead of promoting the use of cleaner substitutes. Besides, its removal allows the government to redirect public funds (for example, increasing spending on education and health).

According to the price-gap approach, subsidies are calculated as the differential between the price for a good or service in the economy against what that price would be without government intervention. For oil – export countries, though, subsidies do not represent a budgetary impact (if oil prices are fixed over the cost of production, otherwise they have). But importer countries are confronting a different case, with the fisc always assuming the full costs.

Whereas adverse effects are widely recognized, many of the attempts to end the subsidies find mass rejection. In many countries, such a measure breaks with a pre-existing "implicit social contract," which brings an artificially low price to benefit those at the bottom. Henceforth, any attempt to cut fossil fuel subsidies without a plan to compensate the most affected, vulnerable users becomes unsustainable. Inequality issues, though, oblige the policymaker to analyze, in detail, how the measurable impact on the well-being of different consumer groups. In this direction, it is essential to consider both the direct effects (public transport, heating) as well as the indirect ones (on inputs goods and services).

As in many other countries, Ecuador maintained fossil fuels below international prices. Energy subsidies were introduced in the mid-1970s, explaining the social resistance generated after any attempt to eliminate them. To reduce emissions was not primary government objective neither to favor redistributive issues, the cut was part of a package of austerity obligations under a $ 4.2 billion arrangement with the IMF. The package led to a price hike (gasoline rose to $ 0.80 per liter from $ 0.64 per liter), which instigate social revolt. After several days of tension (and, unfortunately, a compelling death toll), the government of Lenin Moreno agreed to eliminate Decree 883.

The precedent paragraphs aim to show how embarrassing it would be to outline energy policies unattended social issues. It might also help to understand how important becomes a political economy framework when analyzing energy transitions. Sometimes opposition to change emerges among those at the bottom, but the demand could also respond to the action of well-organized and reduced groups. A masterplan is needed to break the coalition, to isolate consumers from producers. Subsidies removal should be gradual, implying moving from the present, general configuration to a more specific target scheme.

As an example, take public transport, the largest source of emissions in Latin America[51]. Firstly, by removing general subsidies for fossil fuel, by maintaining them for public transport in the short term. Afterward, by promoting the fleet removal: from old, diesel power buses to new, electrical units. Unthinkable for many, this is the pioneer experience recently initiate in Santiago metropolitan area – Chile. Instead of subsidizing fuel, the Chilean government purchased electric vehicles and leased them to local private operators[52]. Similar experiences were recently launched by the cities of Bogota and Cali, Colombia. From a political perspective, the expansion of electrical buses highlights the innovative role of local authorities in the transition.

3.2.2 The global dimension

At a global level, the introduction of a carbon tax face more significant challenges. If (global) cash transfers are in the conversation, it would be feasible to ignore the origin of the emissions or who should pay for them. A single price for coal would be optimal and widely accepted.

Unfortunately, it is not possible to ignore the existence of market failures, neither to leave ethical considerations aside. Production and consumption occur at the local level, which explains the disinterest of some countries in reducing their pollution effort as well as developed countries' unwillingness to reward new producers for stopping or minimizing pollution. In other words, the decentralized nature explains the disinterest of Mexico in reducing its emissions and the inability of Ecuador to guarantee the Yasuni proposal (see box below). International transfers are difficult to sustain, indeed.

These shortcomings came to explain the impossibility to observe a global, a single price for coal (Chichilnisky and Heal 1994; Chichilnisky, Heal, and Starrett 2000). Remember, if all current fossil fuel reserves are set into operation, what would be used would triple the carbon budget (unburned

---

[51] Whereas at global level public transport explains 18 percent of total emissions, in the region transport represents 31 percent. Is worth to remark that over 80 percent of Latin America citizens resides in urban areas.

[52] The running cost per kilometer of Santiago's Chinese-made electric buses is around 70 pesos ($0.10), a 230-peso decrease on the rate for a diesel vehicle (Reuters "As UN climate talks near, host Chile charges up electric transport" October 9, 2019).

reserves). In order to solve the paradox, quantitative restrictions might be considered an alternative. Governments could agree on a global system of tradable emissions, as established by the Kyoto protocol. However, it did not work (Nordhaus, 2020). The focus here is on the producer's response to the environmental tax.

To analyze the producer's response, a recent contribution from Heal and Schlenker (2019) might be helpful. It combines the ideas of Arthur Cecil Pigou (environmental taxation) with those introduced by Harold Hotelling (tying rents on nonrenewable resources with the market interest rate). Following the Hotelling rule, the arbitrage condition conforms as follows: keeping in the ground vs taking out of the ground.

This states that the firm's financial return (capital gains from leaving the oil in the ground) should equal those emanating from its core business (taking out, selling the oil, and obtaining a return).

Whereas the environmental rate plays a decisive role in reducing CO_2 emissions (make the product more expensive), the interest rate might push for an increase in fossil fuel production (responding to the presence of an income effect, which associates with resource scarcity). The original model assumes interest rate to be constant and exogenous, however, recent contributions recognize the influence of the (biggest) oil producers over international capital markets (van der Meijden, 2015; Pfeiffer, 2017). In other words, producing countries' savings and investment decisions impact the market interest rate, influencing the rate of resource extraction (flow) and the profitability obtained on capital investments (asset motive). Considering both markets simultaneously requires permits to find out who is benefiting from an oil price increase (if producers or importers), as well as, where extraordinary incomes are being directed (to consumption, to savings, or the production of substitutes).[53] In short, when designing a particular climate policy, policymakers should consider the real–financial interaction. Additionally, they should consider the market concentration ratio, as large companies might be able to bypass the carbon tax to customers.[54]

As resources are assumed to be finite (i.e., reflecting the existence of scarcity rents), the imposition of a tax alters the moment of production. Expected green measures might exert more substantial downward pressure

---

[53] The windfall rents obtained by OPEC countries during the 1970s were redirected towards the financial sector. At present, for example, some Middle Eastern producers are redirecting rents to the renewable energy sector.

[54] Note that the presence of cheaper renewable sources, however, reduce oil firms' room for bypass taxes.

on future prices than current ones, hopefully helping reduce emissions. If companies pull forward production, green taxes will not alter the intensity of use, nor will they affect the cumulative level of emissions.[55] Climate change models initially neglected this inter-temporal production pattern; hereafter referred to the "green paradox" by the specialized literature (Sinn, 2008; Gerlagh, 2011). Government influence over oil firm's productive decisions are certainly not a novel idea, but initially raised by Dasgupta, Heal, and Stiglitz (1980): "the effects of tax structure on patterns of extraction are critically dependent on expectations concerning future taxation." Frederick van der Ploeg and Ceese Withagen (2012 and 2015) identify a similar trend, accelerating production, but now emerging from agents' reactions following a sharp decrease in renewable energy costs (or by the generalization of a backstop technology).[56] Replacement imposes a limit (choke) price, above which the demand for traditional fuels becomes null. If the possibility of replacement accelerates (the new technology becoming cheap earlier), it depletes the extra income generated by the environmental tax in the short run, and there is no green paradox. Subsidizing RE, therefore, accelerates the transition (Jaakkola, 2012; Ploeg and Withagen, 2015).

So far, it has been assumed that global oil reserves are homogeneous, whereas, in practice, they are rather heterogenous. Cost differential equates with geographical differentiation, with some producer countries obtaining Ricardian rents and others operating in the margin. For example, oil coming from a conventional field (Saudi Arabia or Venezuela) is less expensive to extract than others extracted from unconventional fields (USA or Argentina). Heterogeneity, then, is decisive when analyzing the effect of introducing a carbon tax. It also is influenced by market structure. In reality, both aspects (degrees of competition and rents) coexist, increasing the complexity of evaluating the carbon tax effect on the rate of extraction pattern. Market turnover implies large financial capacity, and market power allows, for instance, lowering prices in order to block a substitute fuel. Oil companies, however, should not take their rents for granted. As a result of importers' actions, more oil would be kept in the ground.

---

[55] After the announcement, short-term emissions might increase (but total might remain unaltered) (weak). A different situation emerges when both, short-term and total emissions, increases (strong).

[56] The concept refers to a technology that could permanently replace all fossil fuel used on energy production. Introduced by William Nordhaus (1973), it was originally associated with nuclear but it could also refer to any current (PV, solar) or future (unknown) technology, always "resting on a very abundant base."

BOX 2 Phasing Out Oil: The Moral Dimension

As reserves are global, the pool of emissions to be burned is shared. Therefore, the decision regarding which fields should remain unburned becomes complex, involving high economic and social costs. In particular, and after deciding the discontinuity, how should the affected communities be rewarded? What will be producing countries and consuming countries' roles?

As stated, not all production should discontinue, and production will continue for a while. This leads us to inquire about the selection criteria. Should it be based on economic considerations or should social aspects also be valued? Who decides? What resources should be left untapped?

Collier and Venables (2014) adopt a moral dimension, embracing a development perspective (as it asks developed countries to discontinue production first).[57] For them, any (international) attempt to solve the problem (i.e., to phase out carbon emissions) might break down. In negotiating a solution, policymakers should move away from the utilitarian perspective generally adopted to consider fairness, not only economic incentives. Countries are accepting that left reserves be unburned, are sacrificing their rents to provide a public good (i.e., keep emissions unaltered), and some are even providing an "environmental service" (i.e., biosfera conservation). It is fair for them to await compensation.

The Yasuni National Park covers 10,000 sq km of primary rainforest on Ecuador's eastern border with Peru and is reputed to be the biologically richest place on Earth, with more than 200 species of mammals, 550 species of birds, 380 species of fish, and more than 2,000 types of tree. The park is also the ancestral home of three indigenous tribes, the Huaorani, Tagaeri, and Taromenane, who are independent tribes that have resisted all attempts to integrate them into modern life. Beneath this ecological and cultural gem sits another kind of treasure: black gold. In 2007, the Ecuador government proposed to leave the oil in the ground if the international community (partially) compensate the country for lost revenue.[58] The Yasuni initiative brings an opportunity to transition to

---

[57] Collier and Venables (2014) deals with the phasing out of coal, considering that countries' response depends on economic incentives but also on moral pressure

[58] The Ecuadorian government asked the international community to compensate it ($3.6 bn) for lost revenue ($7,2 bn). In order to signal its commitment, in conjunction with the United Nations, the Ecuadorian government established a trust fund and promised to compensate donors if the original pledge were broke. This fund was established to accept contributions from governments, private entities, and nongovernmental organizations.

a post-oil development model, somehow in line with Collier and Venables' proposal.

However, on August 15, 2013, the Ecuadorian government decided to end the initiative and open the Yasuni Park to extract oil. According to the government, the decision followed the lack of enthusiasm generated by the initiative. The Yasuni–ITT was considered a defeat for conservation activists and organizations, with no agreement on the ultimate causes of it (Martin and Scholz, 2014; Larrea and Murmis, 2018). The failure, however, should not debase the supply-side policy role (Harstad, 2012; Collier and Venables, 2014; Bucaram et al., 2017; Larrea and Murmis, 2018; Tudela, 2018; Codato et al., 2019). It avoids free-riding issues presented by demand-driven policies and leading to the green paradox. Supply alternatives, however, require raising funds, and that is where the problems arise. Alternatively, countries could unilaterally declare a moratorium: prohibiting oil exploration activities at a national level (Costa Rica) or banning them in a particular area (Mexico and Belize) (Tudela, 2018). Independent of the funding, in addition to preserving biodiversity and benefiting indigenous peoples, this type of unilateral measure helps maintain the carbon budget.

Once the moratorium is declared, a ring-fence is on place: an unburnable carbon area emerges. The magnitude of the challenge force to define a transitional path, preferentially, rushing to protect those areas of the most considerable conservation value (Lessman et al., 2016; Larrea and Murmis, 2018; Codato et al., 2019). Priority should go to those areas of greater biodiversity and cultural value, with geographical criteria focusing on highly sensitive areas of global heritage. The phasing-out strategy adopts a bottom-up, local focus approach, prioritizing social and environmental gains over economic considerations (Schoenmaker and Schramade, 2019). In sum, oil exploitation in the Amazons is incompatible with the carbon budget (Amazon Watch, 2020), but it also entails a moral dilemma (Collier and Venables, 2014).

In practice, political decisions escape from purely economic and moral issues, to involve economic interests and geopolitical aspects. As an example, consider the Amazon rainforest, which provides a set of essential ecosystem services to the world but remains under threat. Despite the millionaire environmental campaigns or CSR statements, transnational banks and investment funds continue to finance oil exploitation in the Amazon (Amazon Watch, 2020]. Likewise, consider oil sand exploitation, which is not economically viable while showing a high environmental cost. Even so, both the USA and Canada decided to continue with their respective projects. The same goes for Norway, whose public company continues actively searching for new offshore reserves.[59] That less-developed countries should stop producing is unfair and hypocritical when those more advanced decide to move forward with exploration tasks (Jaffe, 2020; www.lofotendeclaration.org/#read).

3.3 Climate Change and Sustainable Development: Making the Invisibile More Detectable

In discussing climate change and greenhouse emissions stocks, the historical responsibility of developed countries (DCs) is widely accepted. It explains less developed countries' (LDCs) claim for compensation. Nevertheless, the rise of a group of emerging economies generated a significant increase in the level of emissions (flows).

The protocol agreed in Kyoto set a dual mitigation strategy: DCs assuming the burden, LDCs left without responsibilities. Whereas some DCs assumed ambitious commitments to curb emission levels (production), savings were then neutralized by high carbon imports (Aichele and Felbermayr, 2011). Globalization stabilized emissions in the North, but those originating in the South increased. A significant boost in pollution levels and the interconnected health problems led China to recognize the relevance of the challenge. Then, the COP 21 at Paris introduced a bottom-up approach that calls participants to offer their contributions (NDCs) to tackle the problem. Whereas it reminds all participants' countries of the need to take action, it does not either prescribe specific actions or impose sanctions for those breaking the promises.

With globalization expanding to unprecedented levels, maintaining past production at the heart of the analysis proved inaccurate. International trade brought back the South–North debate (Davis et al., 2010; Peters et al., 2011). Those living in affluent societies feel no guilt, and often do not feel the consequences of their consumption behavior. Perceived as unfair, a group of

---

[59] Self-proclaimed as an (environmentally) conscious global player, Norway proposed to advance with the original 2050 commitment in Paris to 2030. At the same time, however, Equinox (former Statoil) moved forward with the exploration of its reserves in the North Sea (*New York Times*, June 17, 2017, "Both Climate Leader and Oil Giant? The Norwegian Paradox").

authors decided to advance with a new approach, now focused on consumption – the "carbon footprint" that accounts for emissions according to the place of consumption. The proposed scheme includes an ethical response. Whatever the case, whereas a local response can be attained, to determine a global resolution remains complex.

Latin American's global insertion pattern is slightly different, as wealth creation associates with natural resources exploitation (Muradian et al., 2012; Schaffartzik et al., 2014). Although biomass and metals are often portrayed with the regional (material) export basket, the region is also a net exporter of fossil energy. Indeed, as in any production process, an essential share of exported resources are consumed or dissipated in the process. Think about waste pits contaminated with oil; gas vented or oil leaked through the pipeline (Sinnott et al., 2010). Beyond the (economic) costs generated during the process, the social and environmental damage remains misreported under the traditional cost–benefit analysis (Zarsky and Stanley, 2013; Cardoso, 2015).

Export volumes involve a vast amount of resources whose costs are not accounted for by the firm nor recorded by national accounts. An alternative accounting route is to use the material flow accounting framework (MFA) (Lutter et al., 2016; UNEP, 2016). Several countries around the world are starting to include material use and material efficiency assessments, as part of a green growth strategy. However, relying on domestic material consumption (DMC) might be misplaced as the indicator does not account for the use of upstream raw materials. In short, MFA accounting follows a production rather than a consumption-based perspective. As such, it leaves the environmental burden on producer countries (Giljum, 2004; Giljum and Eisenmenger, 2004). In order to overcome this, a group of authors propose another indicator, the "material footprint" (MF) (Weidmann et al., 2013; Giljum et al., 2014; Lutter et al., 2016). MF considers all raw materials used along the value chain, including those being discarded in the production process, thus accounting for the total environmental impact of the production process. By considering all raw materials used to generate a tonnage of export, those using the MF framework would be reporting larger volumes compared to those using the MFA-DMC one (Figure 2).

All productive processes have environmental consequences for the producer country; however, those relying on raw material production are the most exposed. Among them, a decline in export prices pushes the environmental burden ever further (as observed in the aftermath of every crisis). There is a consensus that the export-led developmental path leads to more natural

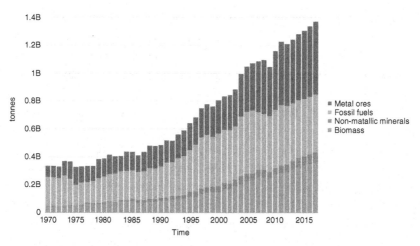

Figure 2 Exports of Latin America + the Caribbean in 1970–2017, by material group

Source: Reference-Disclaimer: WU Vienna (2019): Comparing different indicators for selected country/region. Visualisation based upon the UN IRP Global Material Flows Database. Vienna University of Economics and Business: materialflows.net/visualisation-centre

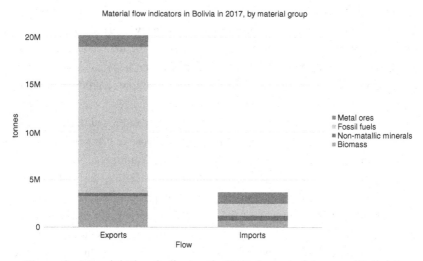

Figure 3a Material Flow indicators in 2017, by material group (Bolivia)

resource depletion, environmental pollution, and social conflict. In the case of fossil fuel exporters, the push generates a direct increase in CO_2 emissions.

Figures 3a to 3e show the material flow export and import indicators for a group of select fossil fuel producer countries in Latin America. In almost all

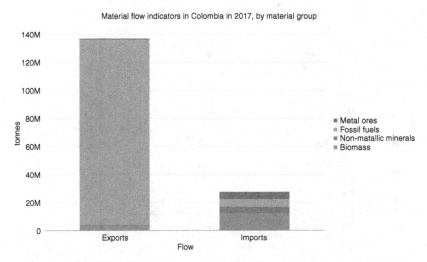

Figure 3b Material Flow indicators in 2017, by material group (Colombia)

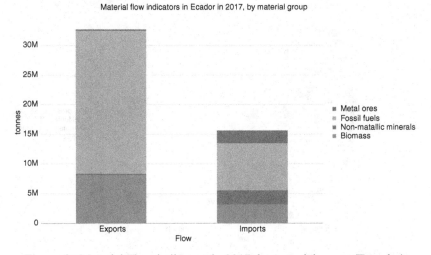

Figure 3c Material Flow indicators in 2017, by material group (Ecuador)

of them, the export baskets of these countries appear highly concentrated. From an economic perspective, this implies being exposed to volatility.

From a quantitative perspective, material flows compare tonnes of exports and imports. When the value of a tonne of export decreases, the country is forced to get behind a more significant physical trade deficit (PTDs). An unequal ecological exchange (Samaniego et al., 2017), which somehow complements the unequal exchange theory, is associated with the Singer-Prebisch

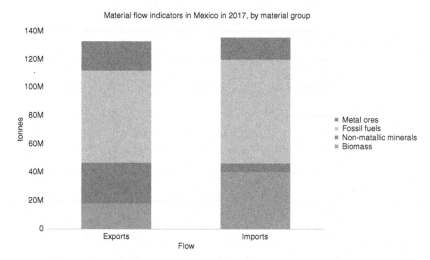

Figure 3d Material Flow indicators in 2017, by material group (Mexico)

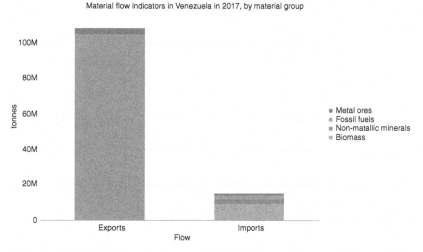

Figure 3e Material Flow indicators in 2017, by material group (Venezuela)
Source: Reference-Disclaimer: WU Vienna (2019): Comparing different indicators for selected country/region. Visualisation based upon the UN IRP Global Material Flows Database. Vienna University of Economics and Business: materialflows.net/visualisation-centre

thesis (Pérez-Rincon, 2006; Ciplet and Roberts, 2017; Givens et al., 2019). Prebisch deterioration of the terms of trade concept combines the adverse effects of the low-income elasticity of raw material demand with the presence of asymmetries in the labor market's functioning.

López (2010) and Barbier (2015) arrive at a similar conclusion but approach from a different angle. Both remark on the relevance of natural capital in Latin America's development, a concept neglected by the traditional national account framework.[60] By disregarding all the externalities associated with natural resource exploitation, natural assets go undervalued. Consequently, undervaluation perpetuates a structural imbalance (Barbier, 2015, p. 9). The region also underinvests in human capital (health, skills, and education), perpetuating the dual character of the economy. Wealth creation among developed and newly industrialized countries, by contrast, associates with the production of skill-intensive goods. As human capital is scarce in the aggregate, skill-trained workers obtain a premium wage. Global commodity markets allow industrialized countries to keep expanding, alongside perpetuating a structural imbalance in their favor. For Latin American countries, this trend implies equating economic development with resource depletion and pollution, altering local ecosystems. There is a need for exploitation to increase to maintain economic growth, reducing and degrading natural resource endowment.

4 Energy Transition: Macroeconomic, Development and Geopolitical Challenges

To date, several studies have validated the anthropogenic character of climate change, with dire consequences for the planet's human and nonhuman lives. The magnitude of the challenge cannot go unnoticed by those in charge of macroeconomic affairs, particularly among policymakers in the South. It is time to ask: which policies should and could be adopted, and which policy instruments are available to the ruler?

For fossil fuel producer countries, macro challenges will come, and simultaneously affect its fiscal and external fronts. As explained earlier, producers might be forced to leave a large part of their reserves in the ground. More pressure could follow if a "peak demand" strike looks near, conducting to nonrenewable assets devaluation (Covert et al., 2016; Dale and Fatouh, 2017).[61] It remains unknown how fast the deceleration process will be, but specialists agree that the peak might be closer than expected. Nevertheless, oil

---

[60] The reductionist vision embedded in the national account framework (physical capital) dates from the industrial revolution, whose profound economic structural transformation came to change the composition of capital and thus redefined wealth. This redefinition has important implications for how we view nature, and especially natural and ecological capital (Barbier, 2015, p. 32).

[61] The explosive growth in wind and solar sources is behind the demand for fossil fuel peak, a situation increasing the likelihood of a carbon bubble. In a recent report, Carbon Tracker foresaw the global demand peaking in the mid 2020s (Carbon Tracker, 2018b).

producer countries keep investing in new exploration projects – the "carbon entanglement" problem. As rents are still around, Norway and Mexico both have interests in obtaining a significant stake in global fossil fuel markets (OECD, 2013; Erickson et al., 2015).

This Section starts with describing the macroeconomic challenges imposed by the transition among fossil fuel exporter countries (Section 4.1). Then, it presents the monetary policy role in combating climate change (Section 4.2). However, besides financial norms and regulations, nothing guarantees a long-term vision from bankers. Accordingly, and because of the small size of the financial system, it might be worth to rethink development banks' role in energy transition (Section 4.3). Finally, Section 4.4 analyzes the state's role and the relevance of having a strategic vision.

4.1 Latin America, Economic Policy, and Climate Change: The Art of the Possible

Energy transition implies a process of structural change, with significant effects on the national economy (Ocampo, 2011). The magnitude of the change is even more significant among oil-exporting countries, as the movement adds new macro adversities and challenges. What is striking among fossil fuel producers, summarized in a couple of indicators (Tables 4 and 5; and Figure 4), is how natural resource dependence endured.

The global transition towards a green, renewable energy source will alter the historical (brown, nonrenewable) global insertion pattern. To some extent, none of these countries see the climatic problem as alien to the productive model, a somewhat dystopian view, although observed even among developed countries (for example, consider Canada's tar sands project). However, Latin American countries have a lower capacity, less political space for reaction, and fewer funds for mitigation.

Awareness of such specificity means development discussions should focus on how to start the decarbonization trend. Disadvantages do not associate only with financial resources, as funds are still arriving, but also on how they are distributed (Section 4.3). The neoliberal discourse remains a cornerstone of Latin America's international insertion, relying on a static comparative model and a traditional, neoliberal finance viewpoint. In addition, the oil industry lobby undermines any attempt at change. In other words, a mix of political weaknesses and ideological prejudices prevents any progress towards a strategy of productive diversification.

When countries' global insertion associates with the exploitation of nonrenewable resources, then national economies are exposed to, simultaneously, saving and fiscal and external gaps. Widely recognized by those working at the

Table 4 Oil rents to GDP, select countries (2002–17)

Country Name	2002	2003	2004	2005	2006	2007	2008	2009	2010	2011	2012	2013	2014	2015	2016	2017
Bolivia	2.64	3.32	4.81	7.25	6.87	6.21	6.34	2.64	3.44	4.45	4.45	4.26	3.81	1.32	0.93	1.32
Colombia	3.40	3.88	4.11	4.95	5.32	4.26	5.48	3.25	4.44	6.81	6.13	5.80	5.29	2.74	1.84	2.67
Ecuador	7.91	8.79	13.07	17.50	18.48	16.57	18.43	8.77	11.18	15.67	13.82	12.58	11.07	4.36	3.18	4.96
Mexico	2.50	3.33	4.18	5.50	5.70	5.11	5.98	3.41	4.11	5.61	5.34	4.72	3.93	1.61	1.22	1.72
Venezuela, RB	17.17	19.88	25.17	30.11	28.86	20.22	20.50	9.92	11.84	22.70	17.72	17.07	11.29	N/D	N/D	N/D

Source: World Bank (DATABASE)

Table 5 Fossil fuel related fiscal incomes, selected countries

Country	2000–3	2005–8	2010–14	2015–17
Argentina	0.8%	1.6%	1.0%	1.2%
Bolivia	2.7%	9.1%	10.6%	6.8%
Brazil	0.8%	1.2%	0.8%	0.9%
Colombia	1.6%	2.4%	3.4%	1.4%
Ecuador	5.7%	8.7%	12.8%	5.8%
Mexico	3.0%	1.1%	1.4%	5.1%
Trinidad and Tobago	7.6%	16.2%	12.4%	4.9%
Venezuela	10.5%	13.8%	9.9%	n/a

Source: own elaboration based on Gomez Sabaini et al. (2017) and OECD (2019)

Figure 4 Fossil fuel exports (% of merchandise exports) (2018)
Source: World Development Institute

structuralist and heterodox traditions (Ocampo, Rada, and Taylor, 2009), the macro relevance of these constraints has recently gained IMF attention (Clayton and Levi, 2015; Sester and Frank, 2017). Since 2008, the Fund started to evaluate fiscal breakeven oil prices (FBOP) for a group of oil producer countries. Different authors and market analysts have recently started to follow a new indicator: the external breakeven oil price (EBOP) metric.[62] The national

---

[62] The FBOP confers the minimum oil price governments need to meet their spending commitments while balancing their budgets. A similar rule could be found for the current account, with the EBOP evaluating the minimum oil price needed to meet the country's external payments

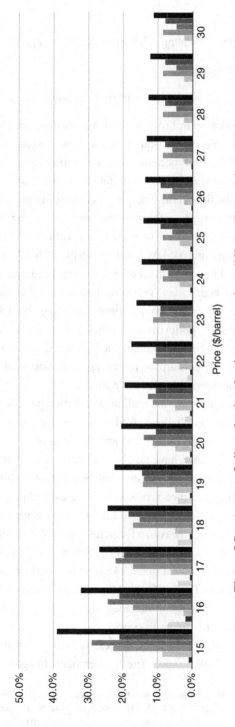

Figure 5 Percentage of oil production that is uneconomic at different Brent prices, 2020

Source: own elaboration based on IEA and BP

account framework permits us to observe how macro components and restrictions are interconnected:

(Investments – Savings) + (Public Spending – Taxes) + (Exports – Imports) = 0

Alternatively, consider the following identity:

Private Sector Deficit + Fiscal Deficit = Net External Borrowing

The balance of payments plays a central role in Latin American economies, exhibiting short-term macro implications, and long-standing development effects. The "dominant" role of the BOP became even bolder after the 1970s, as one country after another decided to liberalize its financial sector so as to open their capital account. Add the financialization process initiated in the early 2000s by the (oil and gas) industry, transforming the investment decision process of non-financial companies, and oil now trades as a financial asset (Cheng and Xiong, 2013; Adams and Glück, 2014; Vercelli, 2014).[63] The presence of highly volatile capital flows has induced more pronounced cyclical shocks, reinforcing the national economies' procyclical character. The new macro context severely reduced sovereign policy space, including room for anti-cyclical policies. Unfortunately, policymakers' room to smooth private consumption or to prevent a surge in imports is undoubtedly limited, so, during a boom and despite the presence of fiscal surplus, private agent decisions might drive the economy towards a net external borrowing position.

Procyclical capital flows have reinforced the traditional insertion pattern not to diversify the economy. However, the challenge for Latin American countries goes beyond the prescribed alert to avoid the cyclical and recurrent BOP crisis. Crude oil might, sooner rather than later, have no physical markets to trade (a large portion of LA reserves might soon become stranded - see Figure 5). If the provisions made at Paris are maintained, then Venezuela should leave 95 percent of its extra-heavy reserves unburnable (McGlade and Etkins, 2015). Before the ban occurs, the peak demand to arrive; however, a financial crisis will materialize. As the present situation testifies, with the Brent barrel below $20, the recession might be around the corner: at that price, 14 percent of total production [1,2 (Mb/day)] turns uneconomic (Figure 6). This (sudden and unexpected) sharp fall in price made all gaps emerge simultaneously. Oil-related fiscal incomes are in jeopardy right now; the future has come.

The sharp price decline represents a 50 to 80 percent reduction in public coffers, so more fiscal stress will come. The government budgets of

---

[63] Financialization captures the increasing exposure of oil as other commodities through a variety of instruments (futures, options, exchange-traded funds) by a comprehensive set of market participants (such as hedge funds, pension funds, insurance companies, and retail investors).

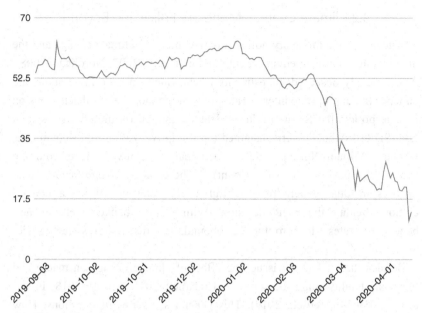

Figure 6 WTI oil crude daily prices (2019-Sep-03 to 2020-Apr-22)
Source: Macrotrends Data Download

Venezuela, Ecuador, and, to a lesser extent, Colombia rely heavily on oil taxes, royalties, and sales. With estimated breakeven fiscal prices above USD 100, all of them are in dire fiscal straits. However, as a traditional oil producer but a more diversified economy, the fiscal breakeven price for Mexico remained affordable at USD 50; it will be different if the oil price stumbles. The room for fossil fuel subsidies shrinks, with the cut now affecting producers all around the region. Otherwise, the government would be forced to augment its public debt. A consensus is emerging among some groups of investors asking governments not to bail out industries or business models that are not in line with the coming low-carbon world (March 26, 2020, by Michael Liebreich Senior Contributor BloombergNEFI Liebrich. COVID - 19: The Low Carbon Crisis. March 26, 2020 https://about.bnef.com/blog/covid-19-the-low-carbon-crisis/), and to attach subsidies only to those companies having a detailed decarbonization plan (FT, 2020a).

What is needed is a structural transformation to explore new alternatives for development and the sooner they began to work on the design of this structural transformation, the better. To facilitate a smooth transition, the state should delineate macro (fiscal, monetary, and exchange rate) and developmental policies. A long-term, strategic vision is also needed. While aware of these shortcomings and the alerts coming from the scientific community, policymakers continue to bet on the extractive model.

4.2 Climate Change, Monetary Policy and Beyond

Consider now the monetary policy role in combating climate change and the interest rate impact on environmental policy (Stern, 2007; Nordhaus, 2008). As previously observed, investments in abatement involve large sums and patience (an appropriate interest rate). One of the most heated discussions on climate policy, the Stern-Nordhaus debate centered on the social discount rate (SDR). Nicholas Stern sustained a prescriptive, zero pure discount rate, whereas William Nordhaus defended a real descriptive time discounting approach (a positive rate of discount).[64] The choice has significant consequences on future generations, highlighting the relevance of ethical considerations behind the SDR decision. With central bankers setting their benchmark rates close to the zero-bound, the discussion somehow de-escalated[65].

Besides the rate-setting issue, the effect of climate change on macro and financial stability might be substantial (Carney, 2015; Coeuré 2018; Frisari et al., 2019; Rudebusch, 2019). This generates a series of questions: How does climate change affect the financial system? What was (and what might be) the response of the monetary authority to such a situation? What are the policy instruments available? What kind of regulations are appropriate?

The first question led to evaluating the risks generated by climate change: physical and transition (see Section 2.2), as we have mentioned. From a financial perspective, though, the system risks associated with a too-rapid movement towards a low-carbon economy could materially damage financial stability. For monetary authorities in fossil fuel exports in developing countries, the risk of transition becomes more compelling. Moreover, they should pay attention to future scenarios and demand peak prospects.

About the second question, the truth is that monetary policy continued to be marked by a narrow-minded approach (Campiglio et al., 2018; D'Orazio and Popoyan, 2018; Fischer and Alexander, 2019; Vercelli, 2019). As an example, consider the FED Quantitative Easing program (QE). This program was not only degraded by banks in financing the payment of awards to their management cadres but also favored the purchase of corporate bonds issued by carbon-intensive companies. A similar bias has been followed by the European Central Bank, favoring brown industries in both its current asset purchase

---

[64] The interest rate differential explains the divergence in environmental tax values per tonne of CO_2 (Nordhaus \$8, Stern \$85). Surprisingly, the former look close to the worldwide average whereas the latest value is close to the IMF suggested value (Section 3.2).

[65] Under the normative approach, SDR differs from market interest rates, whereas in the prescriptive approach both are equal.

practices but also in its collateral framework and haircut regime (FT, 2018[66]; Chenen et al., 2019). Given its historical legacy, financial system liquidity has ended up favoring carbon-intensive investments. All this forces us to rethink the objectives, functions, and policies pursued by central banks around the world. If we understand that attacking climate change results in the main problem to be solved by the present generation, then the sovereign must design any policy and use every instrument at his disposal to accomplish that objective. In this sense, the monetary authority must look at the very long term and place their policies therein, as future generations can take advantage of their patience. Based on all this, perhaps the time has come to rethink the monetary instruments as well as to redesign financial regulation to pursue the enormous challenges posed by climate change.

Concerning the last question, the central bank has several options. Authorities could force financial institutions to assess environmental risks when granting a loan: transparent the risks generated by climate change and those arising from mitigation policies. In order to reduce the present bias and to contain the destabilizing effect of fossil fuel investments, the monetary authority should classify the "brown" risk attached to a specific loan, and thus measure the degree of risk the commercial bank is assuming with the operation. Likewise, the bank could set a limit on the total volume of loans directed to oil and related brown industries (or directly ban them) (Chenen et al., 2019). This differentiation, although banning, serves to demonstrate the risk involved in investing in assets that will lose their value. It can also introduce "green" guidelines. With the same objective, the reserve requirement for "green" credits could be reduced, in turn reducing the financial cost of the loan. Another way of influencing the portfolio of banks would be to evaluate the instruments used as collateral. At the micro-prudential level, in short, authorities should be pushing financial institutions to evaluate the environmental risks properly.

Central bankers could go beyond, and implement a "green" QE (Campliglio et al., 2018; Fischer and Alexander, 2019), or stimulate the green bond market (Haldane, 2011 and 2013; Thanassoulis, 2014; Gersbach and Rochet, 2017; Knot, 2018). These actions affect the balance sheet of the central bank, making it "greener." The fact that benchmark interest rates are close to the zero-bound level is helpful, permitting governments to introduce climate policies with negative interest rates (Fleurbaey and Zuber, 2013). All the proposed actions should bring a developmental spirit and an active attitude of the monetary authority to guarantee the transition (Dafe and Voltz, 2015).

The relevance of monetary tools, however, decays among LDCs. Firstly, this is because of their reduced policy space. Secondly, even those profiting from some

---

[66] "BoE itself must now take action on climate change" Letter, from Daniela Gabor and others. *Financial Times*. November 14, 2018, www.ft.com/content/269af14a-e678-11e8-8a85-04b8afea6ea3.

room might be unable to fund climate policies because of high financial costs (interest rate gap), and exchange rate dynamics. Last but not least is the minor role of the local financial market in oil and gas industry funding. Big oil companies' projects are financed through equity either by debt raised at international financial centers (bonds) or obtained from (bilateral or multilateral) developmental banks (credits). Henceforth, policymaker attention should be placed on cross-border capital flows rather than (only) concentrating on local banks' credit practices. Governments, then, should consider alternatives and command and control instruments.[67] Some macro-prudential tools (Bolton et al., 2020) build upon the "precautionary principle" proposed by Taleb and associates (2014) and reflected by Chenet, Ray-Collins, and van Lerven (2019) for the financial sector in dealing with climate change risks.

Controls are not envisioned as usual macro tools (to reduce exchange rate volatility or for the effects of incoming flows on the competitiveness of the exchange rate or to incentivize industrialization. Controls are envisioned here to avoid overinvestments in the nonrenewable sector. A prudent regulation is envisioned to avoid a "fossil fuel bubble," not to deter a particular type of foreign direct (brown) investments – although it could be the case. As price-takers and marginal suppliers, Latin American countries are incapable of influencing global transition dynamics. Regional players, however, could be positively affected by a rapid movement towards a low-carbon economy and observe serious damage to their local financial systems. Henceforth, this prudent measure is set to avoid "the risk of a more abrupt and widespread correction in financial markets as the financial risks from climate change are re-evaluated" (Bank of England, 2018, p. 24). Otherwise, an asset revaluation "could destabilize markets, spark a procyclical crystallization of losses and lead to a persistent tightening of financial conditions: an environmental, Minsky moment" (Carney, 2016, p. 2).

Policymakers should also be aware that not all foreign direct investment (FDI) flows are beneficial for the economy, and may not be desirable for the country's long-term sustainable development. For instance, fossil fuel related FDI flows could come to alter pristine, unique ecosystems, so the sovereign should set aside the permissive, traditional regulatory vision regarding FDI followed up to now. It should abandon the quantitative vision and adopt a qualitative perspective instead (Sauvant and Mann, 2017). Not all investments favor sustainable development,[68]

---

[67] The task should be at the highest level, though, not left in the hands of (independent) monetary authorities.

[68] The Rio Declaration on Environment and Development presents it as follows: "In order to protect the environment, the precautionary approach shall be widely applied by States according to their capabilities. Where there are threats of serious or irreversible damage, lack of full scientific certainty shall not be used as a reason for postponing cost-effective measures to prevent environmental degradation."

with many projects ending up being socially expensive and environmentally damaging. Therefore, and to evaluate (capital) inflows, the government would benefit from using the project material footprint approach. In any case, a new type of agreement could be established on currently approved projects and operating coal power plants (to avoid costly international litigations),[69] although prohibiting the arrival of funds for the new ones. Oil producer countries, however, should be (somehow) recompensed as the moratoria are going to affect the local economy. On the other hand, they should induce the entry of long-term capital, basically oriented towards financing a new, sustainable infrastructure network. Industrialized countries could also help accelerate the trend by bringing funds (Section 4.3) and by favoring the transfer of technology (Section 4.4).

4.3 Financing for Development and the Public Financing of the New (Old) Energy Matrix

Access to long-term financing flows might be difficult (if not impossible) for developing countries, a failure recognized by Thomas Veblen, John M. Keynes, or Hyman Minsky (Mazzucato, 2013). In the past, local elites assimilated the failure and decided to establish a new institutional "patient investor": public development banks (PDBs). Unfortunately, around the 1990s, PDBs started to lose relevance throughout the world. The international financial crisis would renew interest in them (Studart and Gallagher, 2016).

Developmental problems not only persist, but social and environmental costs have to keep growing. The challenges imposed by climate change are even more significant. Indeed, because of its greater exposure, developing countries and emerging economies will have to confront considerable investments in mitigation and adaptation. The need for long-term financial flows is compelling as ever. So far, the region continues to attract foreign investors, including direct investment flows for long-term, capital-intensive projects. Unfortunately, inflows are not financing the transition but deepening the extractive, nonrenewable model (Samaniego et al., 2017; Zhou et al., 2018; DeAngelis and Tucker, 2020; Jaffe, 2020; Stanley, 2020).

The financing for development problems, if any, does not associate with short-termism funding (Mazzucato, 2015; Schoenmaker and Schramade, 2019), but with funds' sectoral composition. One of the limitations is the voluntary approach adopted at the regulatory level (NFGS), whose influence on investment and bank lending behavior is minimal (Christophers, 2017; Ameli et al., 2019; Chenet et al., 2019). Nongovernment agencies are also

---

[69] As observed in the Netherlands, whose the government decision to shut down coal plants by 2030 generated an investment treaty claim (IISD, 2019).

very critical of private banks and institutional investors, as they continue to provide loans to oil and gas (RainForest Network, 2019; Amazon Watch, 2020). Critics have also argued that the problems originate not only in the private sector, but that, regrettably, an essential part originates from multilateral banks, export credit agencies, and public financial entities (ODI – OCI, 2015; Christianson et al., 2017; Oil Change International, 2017; DeAngelis and Tucker, 2020). To name a case, think of loans granted by Chinese policy banks acting in the region. In this sense, a recent study by Yuan and Gallagher (2018) suggests that a little more than two-thirds of the funds that arrived during the period 2003–16 went to finance the oil industry and to the creation of infrastructure supporting it (whereas the green sector was favored by 17 - percent).[70] A similar tale comes from multilateral banks, which, except for the European Investment Bank, overwhelmingly remains at fault to their original pledge; namely, to align operations with the mitigation and adaptation goals originated at the Paris Agreement (Fekete et al., 2020). For example, consider the World Bank Group (WBG). As stated in several discourses and proposals, the WBG committed to allocate its funds to better finance the transition towards a green economy. It continues to finance fossil fuel projects and, until recently, even the high-pollutant coal industry (Wright et al., 2017; Mainhart, 2019). If the carbon-biased pattern keeps prevailing, the ensuing technological lock-in will harm Latin American countries for several years.

Opposition to non-energy funding, however, keeps growing. New developmental values are essential. Development banks can, without a doubt, help in the finance of the green infrastructure and the move towards a technologically sustainable "lock-in" (Griffith-Jones et al., 2020).

Despite everything, much remains to be done (and financers of it found). Not only should the funds be used to solve the problems that climate change entails, but it should also make development sustainable.

4.4 Energy Transition Geopolitical Challenges

The magnitude of the challenge brought about by climate change and energy transition exceeds the economic dimension; its geopolitical consequences are even more critical (Morris, 2016; O'Sullivan et al., 2017; WEC, 2018; Bonnet et al., 2019; Carcagane, 2019; Stevens, 2019; Malcomson, 2020). From a strategic perspective, energy policy design includes four axes: availability, accessibility, affordability, and acceptability. The World Energy Council adopts, somehow, a similar perspective. Since 2010, this entity has presented the energy

---

[70] An important share goes to the funding of hydroelectric dams, projects with high environmental and social costs.

trilemma, contemplating energy security, equity in access, and environmental sustainability (Goldthau and Sovacool, 2012; Gunningham, 2013; Heffron et al., 2015; Wixforth and Hoffmann, 2019). Whatever the metric being considered, renewable sources are displacing nonrenewable.

So far, we have mentioned the different factors that triggered the transition (changes in relative prices, higher energy efficiency, new regulations), as well as the irreversible character of the transition. However, the length of the transition remains uncertain (Fouquet, 2010; Sovacool, 2016). As mentioned, the shorter the period, the more extensive the (transitional) risks. Under a business-as-usual scenario, though, physical risks augment. What will be the speed with which developed countries and large emerging economies (driven by demand energy) complete the transition process is uncertain (but it could move closer). Thus, governments in Latin America must confront the challenges whose resolution implies acting in the short, medium, and long term.

Policymakers should work on the transition, putting social cohesion at the forefront. In parallel, authorities should keep an eye on economic diversification, aiming to install a new model of inclusive and sustainable development. The world is rapidly moving from an energy model based on molecules to another based on electrons, with countries betting on technological development leading the change. The "race for the energy of the future" forces us to review the role played by the state, undoubtedly decisive in the rapid expansion evidenced by this industry after the global financial crisis (Capriotti, 2009; Kalamova et al., 2011; Lewis, 2011; Kuntze and Moerenhout, 2013; Mazzucato, 2013 and 2015; Dent, 2014; Kim and Thurbon, 2015; Chen and Lees, 2016; Lapachelle et al., 2017; Mazzucato and Semienuik, 2018; Bonnet et al., 2019; Chien, 2019; Hansen et al., 2019).[71]

Less developed, energy-dependent countries should profit from the opportunities that renewable energies bring for long-term, sustainable development. As promising as these attributes might be from a societal perspective, technical knowledge permits laggards to climb the ladder. Intangible goods, though, are now appreciated as the new geopolitical assets. Henceforth, and in order for dividends to be attained, governments should (properly) design the transition. State participation can be direct and in one or more of the value chain segments. However, it can also be indirect, through the support of the private sector via financial transfers, differentiated tax treatment, infrastructure provision, energy regulation, or based on the granting of guarantees and subsidies. Empirically,

---

[71] A similar statement could be made concerning the race for the automotive of the future (Tillemann, 2015) or the one behind lithium battery (Levine, 2015)

however, we observe a continuous line, with the public sector playing a crucial role in the R&D phase. The private sector often has a significant role in the production and distribution phases. Notwithstanding, a different picture emerges among Southeast Asian nations, where the state played a leading role (Dent, 2014; Kim and Thurbon, 2015; Chien, 2019; Thurbon, 2019).

Consider next the RE role for advancing in the value chain, and the options available. So far, Latin American countries have disregarded the power of auctions, FITs, or similar schemes to further advance the industrialization cum research process (Lapachellle et al., 2017). Despite being beneficial, by denying technological aspects, (large) auction scheme projects create dependence. When designing auctions, though, governments should articulate policies taking into account industrial drivers and intellectual property rights issues (Bonne et al., 2019). If the government's objective is to advance in the value chain, previous tender experiences have included technological transfer clauses requiring a certain level of local content. If successful, the program not only induces the establishment of new (mostly foreign) companies but also triggers technological change. China's experience can be considered exemplary, highlighted by the coherence and flexibility that the scheme showed (particularly beneficial in the wind and solar complex development) (Malcomson, 2020). At the regional level, Brazil's experience is instructive: it imposed a 60 percent local content requirement on wind equipment to be purchased from national manufacturers (IRENA, 2013).[72]

In short, the ultimate goal of this type of policy should be to lay the foundations for dynamic competitive advantages. Indeed, many of the technologies actually in use would not be available without prior intervention from the state. However, there is no recipe and no magic potion, describing the role the state should play. Each country must articulate its solution, considering their needs and capabilities – for instance, to assess whether the national industry is ready to confront the task. What the most successful experience comes to show, however, is that the green revolution has not occurred in isolation. Companies all around the world, directly or indirectly, helped China become a technological world leader. Asian authorities have had a strategic, pragmatic vision of developing the renewable industry from scratch (Cheen and Lees, 2016; Chien, 2019; Malcomson, 2020). They are undoubtedly reflecting the widely analyzed Asian developmental model by several scholars (Alice Amsden, Chalmer Johnson, Meredith Woo-Cumings, Robert Wade, or, more recently, Ha-Joon Chang).

Renewable energies are now competitive almost everywhere, a privileged cost position that could place Latin American countries among global leaders.

---

[72] Indeed, the experience has shown the difficulty in meeting the 60 percent local content requirement on equipment in a nascent wind industry in order to receive financing from BNDES. By the time the program started, however, just one Brazilian firm was operative.

Energy transition, however, affects oil and gas companies whose long-term strategic vision has often been remarked. Cornered by critics, though, the world's leading oil companies, whether private or public, have finally decided to begin a transformation process.[73] The idea that prevails in companies' headquarters is that the reign of oil (inexorably) will end, and thus they begin to think of themselves as energy companies. This implies investing in green energy and allocating significant amounts of funds for research and development. Redirection imposes a change of vision, whether initiated by shareholders or imposed by the board of directors. As a result, many leading companies have renewable energy divisions (operating mainly wind and solar PV). In contrast, others initiated an aggressive procurement policy for renewable energy-producing companies and electric utilities.[74] NOCs will also be affected, but some of them are poorly positioned for the clean transition.

Global reserves are largely under NOCs' dominion. Pickl (2019) qualifies oil companies as green (those who aim to become leaders) and blue (laggards). He observes that green attitudes to be mainly observed among those companies with lower reserves in their books. In the regional context, this trend plays unfavorably: the vast proven reserves of companies such as Petrobras, PEMEX, or PDVSA would tend to block any interest in the transition. This bias is aggravated for several reasons, several of which were already mentioned.

Opposition to transition might also originate from shareholders, particularly if they remain attached to traditional business practices and short-term financial objectives. Such is the case of Petrobras, whose traditional investment returns overshadow "green" investment plans. Unsurprisingly, Petrobras' Board of Director's objective remains to increase the firm's competitiveness, which means allocating more resources to exploiting oil resources instead of funding RE projects. Decisions are following the technological expertise that the Brazilian insigne oil company has achieved in offshore exploitation and the reserve potential of pre-salt shows. The company has recently decided to sell its small portfolio of offshore wind assets, in line with Bolsonaro's climate change negations.[75]

---

[73] [Recently] BP pledged to cut its greenhouse gas emissions net-zero by 2050 or sooner, with new chief executive Bernard Looney warning that the oil company had to "reinvent" itself as the world switched to cleaner energy ["New BP boss Bernard Looney pledges net-zero carbon emissions by 2050," FT. February 12, 2020].

[74] A recent report demonstrates, however, that oil and gas companies' investments in renewable energies remain insignificant: 2 percent of total CAPEX expenditures in 2019 ($2.1 billion), (www.iea.org/reports/the-oil-and-gas-industry-in-energy-transitions.

[75] Roberto Castello – Branco, Petrobras chief executive, recently announced that Petrobras was exiting from renewables. "Brazilian oil giant Petrobras exits renewables business," Recharge. August 5th, 2018, www.rechargenews.com/transition/brazilian-oil-giant-petrobras-exits-renewables-business/2-1-649136.

There is no silver bullet, however. It is necessary to embrace a broad set of policy tools, combining monetary, prudential, and fiscal policies. However, the challenge could not be solved by an ideal "benevolent social planner," which never existed. The transition should be led by the state, whose strengths and weaknesses should be recognized in advance.[76] Governments, though, should adopt a multidisciplinary, participatory approach while considering national particularities.

5 Conclusions

Climate change is no longer a distant threat: if some tipping points are finally reached, climate and ecosystems might change in abrupt and irreversible ways. Those oil and gas exploration projects affecting biodiversity should be stopped, and right now. The Yasuni experience should be reviewed, and policymakers learn from all their flaws. The "keep oil in the ground" campaign continues to gain supporters, whereas oil and gas companies face a critical challenge as the world increasingly shifts towards clean energy transitions. Peak oil is not a far-distant perspective related to technological advances in oil exploration, but might be close and driven by demand. Expansion and enlargement of the carbon tax are also under analysis; prominent international figures suggest the emergence of a club. These represent a real threat to oil producers countries, of which they remain somehow unaware but certainly unprepared.

Despite physical risks that keep mounting, and some that are already in play, few Latin American countries are properly considering the relevance of physical risks. Instead of stimulating the arrival of foreign firms and funds for mitigation, they remain attached to the neoliberal, business-as-usual finance model. As capital inflows continue to respond to market signals and invest-ors' sentiments, producer countries keep attracting carbon-related flows. In other words, a liberalized capital market induces physical risks to increase. While the switch towards diversification is more urgent than ever, sovereigns keep investing in new projects. Policymakers continue to bet on fossil fuel development, as recently exemplified by Guyana and Suriname. Surprisingly, the World Bank has played a prominent role in financing, and so the double discourse continues (Jaffe, 2020; Stanley, 2020). The arrival of long-term flows might not be rewarding, and they may not be desirable for sustainable development. Overall, the regional view on the FDI issue remains, to some extent, old-fashioned, with a quantitative perspective dominating the invest-ment debate.

---

[76] A call for a non-ideal theory, a Rawlsian type approach dealing with cases of partial Compliance (Caney, 2016).

The other side of the coin, logically, relates to the continuous enlargement of the nonrenewable asset base. Modern financial markets are inherently unstable: "the major flaw of our economy," as Hyman Minsky (2008) noted. As mentioned in the literature review, the closer the world is to the demand peak, the larger the stranded asset risk. Despite being active in networking participation, liberalized financial markets generate bubble-type dynamics, which remains unperceived by Latin America's financial regulators. Instead of looking at cross-border movements, central banks prefer to emulate regulations from industrial countries' financial systems. Obviously, micro-prudential policies should be included in the policy toolkit. To avoid a carbon bubble, however, designing macro-prudential policies would be more appropriate. Authorities might preferentially install capital controls directly if the objective is to prevent the arrival of capitals for some specific sector (coal industry). If no harsh actions are taken, it could be said that financial regulators' inaction would induce the Minsky moment. The impending financial crisis, henceforth, might not qualify as an unknown – unknown episode, but as a "chronicle of a death foretold."

In contrast to the fossil fuel era, tangible property is no longer a geopolitical threat. Natural capital remains undervalued, perpetuating Latin America's structural imbalance. The race for the future connects to intellectual property rights and intangible property, human capital. The end of the oil era, however, could spawn a geopolitical menace for oil producer countries. The effects of the ongoing energy transformation will be significant, affecting the distribution of global power. However, Latin America's peculiarity does not relate to the lack of financial resources because funds (in large amounts) continue to arrive but (mainly) favor the nonrenewable industry.

The energy transition is a subject of analysis and discussion, offering alternative routes and involving a wide range of actors. The social pressure for environmental protection keeps growing, as does the claim for social justice. Indigenous peoples, however, remain invisible and, therefore, unconsulted. The transition might be a helping hand in reversing inequality and bringing the community back in the decision-making process. Technological aspects (scale of operation, greater geographic decentralization, prosumers) and a new institutional setting (regulatory schemes, cooperatives) might turn this ideal into reality. Nevertheless, one of the most critical challenges ahead is behavioural: to introduce a concrete, and consensual, transitional path, a combination of policies that should be publicly disseminated and maintained during the lifespan of the transitional period. A single bullet is not valid, but a combination of policies is likely to be more productive.

This Element showed that a new "green" era is coming, and presents several advantages and challenges: geopolitical advantage, technology leadership, energy security, energy justice, costs, global warming, and pollution. All these factors might, indeed, are placing greener policies on the fora.

5.1 Epilogue

COVID-19 emerged during the writing, so I am finishing this Element following rigorous lookdown measures enacted by the government.

COVID-19 reflects our relationship with nature: biodiversity loss permitting pathogens to break through its natural boundaries. The pandemic is not only generating thousands of deaths around the world, it will spawn considerable social, economic, and political consequences. Perhaps more outstanding, is the assertion that current decisions will shape the world for years to come. It will also set the political context for climate action, hopefully for the better.

COVID-19, above all, should be thought of as an ethical challenge (Wolf, 2020), as is climate change. The human toll might be tremendous, and this is a social disintegration threat that democracies can not afford to leave unattended.

COVID-19 has revived the debate around the role of the state, markets, and communities. It also claims to transform the relationship between the state, markets, and individual choice. Both debates are crucial in shaping climate change dynamics. These debates are undoubtedly interrelated, multidisciplinary, and voicing political, social, and economic issues.

COVID-19 asks for action, a rapid public response. Social distancing became an effective, quick response to stop the virus. Sooner others later, governments around the world started to implement lockdown measures often complemented by testing and other preventive measures. The success might overcome in failure, particularly if the response opens the door to a less democratic society: the militarization and the rise of the digital surveillance state (Galaz, 2020; Harari, 2020; Lanier and Weil, 2020; Wright, 2020). This poses an ethical dilemma for policymakers, particularly for those defending the ideal of individual liberties and democracy. Governments could not just profit from Facebook to control citizens' ideas (either to influence their ideals). Artificial intelligence (IT) allows bureaucrats to track citizens' movements or remotely control the human body temperature, a somehow totalitarian use of technology. The same technology could also profit autocrats in Latin American governments to monitor political opponents, climate change protests, or social activist movements in a remote village in the Andes. Privacy is at stake, as are human rights. Societies, though, could opt for a more cooperative, participatory use of AI to track the pandemic (Mena et al., 2019). Likewise, IT could be used by indigenous communities to detect and report oil liabilities in their territories. What is under discussion goes beyond a technological choice, but whether a democratic, liberal regime should use the new technological advances.

COVID-19 has reinstalled politics center stage, unmasking (charlatan, autocrats) leaders and acknowledging those who have installed a scientific decision-making process. Unscrupulous leaders can manipulate population fears and tighten their grip on power (Nussbaum, 2018). The pandemic could help democracy to either endure or wane. It exposed the relationship between rulers and the governed (Sen, 2020). It also highlights how relevant community involvement remains, reminding us how necessary social capital remains to bringing vigor to liberal democracies. A more democratic, participative democracy is also crucial for guaranteeing a fair and equitable transition.

COVID-19 pushed civil society as well as the scientific community, somehow installing a "social tipping point" (Robinson and Reddy, 2020). It is an opportunity that should also profit climate activists making people aware of our common humanity, and demonstrate how it is actually at risk by the fossil fuel industry. Eventually, this vision will prevail in the post-virus world. But it might not.

COVID19 affects everybody, but is hitting the poorest more (Ahmed et al., 2020; Bottan et al., 2020; Deaton, 2020). Economists' voices are pertinent, therefore, when analyzing related social consequences of the pandemic. The informal sector and unskilled workers are particularly hit (Bergamini, 2020; Sandin, 2020). Wealth inequalities (living conditions, neighborhood quality, access to health system) also deepen the gap. Unfortunately, a similar, unequal picture appears in relation to climate change.

COVID-19 might induce normative and positive effects and long-lasting consequences. The sharpness of the problem requires exceptional responses, and governments' actions should go in this direction. Economic policies should be directed to cope with the foreseen economic crisis, aiming to prevent social breakdowns and avoiding carbon-related industries regaining space in future stimulus packages. It worth remarking that there is no neutral economic stimulus for the climate, nor can the urgency force authorities to abandon fossil fuel projects. The pandemic might also force Latin American governments to implement new fiscal policies as deglobalization prospects force them to redesign the taxing system. A "green exit" to the crisis, additionally, calls for a new approach to macroeconomics.

COVID-19 is also a call for international cooperation, putting multilateralism back on the agenda. It also forces us to rethink globalization, particularly how to tackle the uncooperative legal framework, which still allows the scientific community not "to share knowledge of potential treatments, coordinate clinical trials, develop new models transparently, and publish findings immediately" (Stiglitz et al., 2020). A similar call for international cooperation is valid in order to tackle climate change, notably to ban oil explorations works in Amazonia.

COVID-19 made a normative contribution, bringing the political economy back into the debate. In this sense, the pandemic is acting as a game-changer for governments all around the world. The neoliberal consensus proves outdated (but not obsolete), and the situation calls for "radical reforms," which implies states playing a more active role in the economy [FT, 2020b]. From a developmental perspective, a new vision is necessary. In this Element, we demonstrate how mainstream economists in the finance arena are embracing this common-good viewpoint. Policymakers should redesign the financial system, prioritize long-term funding, and reinstall the "patient investor." Societies should move towards a new growth model, where the state should regain policy space, re-regulate energy markets, and, above all, encourage the participation of new, nonprofit players (cooperatives).

COVID-19 should be thought of as a 100-meter race; climate change as a marathon (Galaz, 2020). Hopefully, the world will win the pandemic race, but humanity should be prepared for the marathon's hardest miles. To win the marathon, we should recognize that a return to "normal" is not an option. Severe, rapid, and consistent action is needed.

References

ACCA (2016). Filling the information black hole: how are financial firms companies reporting the stranded asset risk. The Accounting Chartered Certified Association – ACCA, February.

Adam, Z., & Glück, T. (2014). Financialization in commodity markets: a passing trend or the new normal? University of St. Gallen. Working Paper on Finance N 2014/13.

Ahmed, F. N., Pissarides, C., & Stiglitz, J. (2020). Why inequality could spread COVID-19. Lancet Public Health 2020 – Comment. Published Online April 2, https://doi.org/10.1016/.

Aichele, R., & Felbermayr, G. (2011) : Kyoto and the Carbon Footprint of Nations, Ifo Working Paper, No. 103, Ifo Institute – Leibniz Institute for Economic Research at the University of Munich, Munichand Felbermayr, 2011.

Aigner, R. (2013). Environmental Taxation and Redistribution Concerns. Annual Conference 2013 (Duesseldorf): Competition Policy and Regulation in a Global Economic Order 79859, Verein für Socialpolitik / German Economic Association, https://ideas.repec.org/p/zbw/vfsc13/79859.html.

Amazon Watch. (2020). Investing in Amazon crude: The network of global financiers and oil companies driving the Amazon towards collapse, https://amazonwatch.org/news/2020/0312-investing-in-amazon-crude.

Ameli, N., Drummond, P., Bisaro, A, Grubb, M., & Chenet, H. (2019). Climate finance and disclosure for institutional investors: why transparency is not enough. Climatic Change, https://doi.org/10.1007/s10584-019-02542-2.

Andersson, M., Bolton, P., & Samama F. (2016). Hedging climate risk. Financial Analyst Journal, 72(3): 13–32.

Bank of England. (2015). The impact of climate change on the UK insurance sector: A Climate Change Adaptation Report by the Prudential Regulation Authority. London.

(2018). Transition in thinking: The impact of climate change on the UK banking sector. Report by the Prudential Regulation Authority. London.

Barbier, E. B. (2015).Nature and wealth: Overcoming environmental scarcity and inequality. Palgrave Macmillan.

Battiston, S., Mandel, A., Monasterolo, I., Schutze, F., & Visentin, G. (2017). A climate stress-test of the financial system Nature Climate Change volume 7: 283–288.

Bergamini, E. (2020). How COVID-19 is laying bare inequality. Bruegel – blog post.

Best, R. (2017). Switching towards coal or renewable energy? The effects of financial capital on energy transitions. Australian National University. Mimeo.

Best, R., & Burke, P. J. (2018). Adoption of solar and wind energy: The roles of carbon pricing and aggregate policy support. Australian National University. Crawford School of Public Policy. Centre for Climate Economics and Policy – CCEP Working Paper 1803.

BIS (2019). Turning up the Heat – climate risk assessement in the insurance sector. A report by Patrkck Cleary, William Harding, Jeremy McDaniels, Jean-Phillipe Svoronos, and Jeffery Yong. FSI Insights in Policy Implementation 20.

Böckler, L., & Giannini Pereira M. (2018). Consumer (co-)ownership in renewables in Brazil. In J. Lowitzsch (ed.), Energy transition: Financing consumer co-ownership in renewables. Palgrave Macmillan: 535–580.

Boix, C. (2003). Democracy and redistribution. Cambridge University Press.

Bolton, P., Despres, M., Pereira da Silva, L. A., Saman, F. & Svartzman, R. (2020). The green swan: Central banking and financial stability in the age of climate change. BIS – Banque de France.

Bonnet, C., Carcanague, S., Hache, E., Sokhna Seck G., & Simoën, M. (2019). Vers une Géopolique de l'energie plus complexe? Une analyse prospective tridimensionnelle de la transition énergétique. Energies Nouvelles (EN) – Agence nationale de la recherche (ANR) – l'Institut de relations internationales et stratégiques (IRIS)

Bottan, N., Hoffman, B., & Vera-Cossio, D (2020). Novel dataset reveals the deepening effects of the COVID-19 pandemic on inequality. InterAmerican Development Bank. Ideas Matter – Blogspot, https://blogs .iadb.org/ideas-matter/en/novel-dataset-reveals-the-deepening-effects-of-the-covid-19-pandemic-on-inequality/.

Bozigar, M., Grayb, C. L., & Bilsborrowc, R. E. (2016). Oil extraction and Indigenous livelihoods in the Northern Ecuadorian Amazon. World Development, 78: 125–135.

Bucaram, S., Fernandez, M. Andrés & Grijalva, D. (2016) Sell the oil deposits!: A financial proposal to keep the oil underground in the Yasuni National Park, Ecuador. WIDER Working Paper 2016/14. Helsinki: UNU-WIDER.

Buckley, T. (2019). Over 100 global financial institutions are exiting coal, with more to come: Every two weeks a bank, insurer or lender announces new restrictions on coal. Institute for Energy Economics and Financial Analysis – IEEFA.org.

Caldecott, B. (2017) Introduction to special issue: Stranded assets and the environment, Journal of Sustainable Finance & Investment. 7(1): 1–13

Caldecott, B., Harnett, E., Cojoianu, T., Kok, I., & Pfeiffer A. (2016). Stranded assets: A climate risk challenge. Inter-American Development Bank.

Caldecott, B., Howarth, N., & McSharry, P. (2013). Stranded assets in agriculture: Protecting value from environment-related risks. Smith School of Enterprise and the Environment, University of Oxford.

Campiglio, E., Dafermos, Y., Monnin, P., Ryan-Collins, J., Schotten, G., & Tanaka, M. (2018). Climate change challenges for central banks and financial regulators. Nature Climate Change, 8(6): 462–468. ISSN 1758-678X.

Campos, I., Pontes Luz, G., Marín-González, E., Geahrs, S., Hall, S., & Holstenkamp L. (2020). Regulatory challenges and opportunities for collective renewable energy prosumers in the EU. Energy Policy 138.

Caney, S. (2016). Climate change and non-ideal theory: Six ways of responding to noncompliance. In C. Hewyard and D. Roser (eds.), Climate justice in a non-ideal world. Oxford University Press: 27–41.

Carbon Tracker Initiative. (2018a). Carbon Tracker. 2018. Mind the gap: The $1.6 trillion energy transition risk, www.carbontracker.org/reports/mind-the-gap/.

(2018b). Powering down coal: Navigating the economic and financial risks in the last years of coal power, https://carbontransfer.wpengine.com/wp-content/uploads/2018/12/CTI_Powering_Down_Coal_Report_Nov_2018_4-4.pdf.

(2018c). 2020 vision: Why you should see peak fossil fuels coming, https://carbontracker.org/reports/2020-vision-why-you-should-see-the-fossil-fuel-peak-coming/.

(2019a). Breaking the habit: Why none of the large oil companies are "Paris-aligned", and what they need to do to get there. CTI. Report prepared by Andrew Grant and Mike Coffin.

(2019b). The political tipping point: Why the politics of energy will follow the economics. By Kingsmill Bond.

(2020a). Handbrake turn: The cost of failing to anticipate an Inevitable Policy Response to climate change. CTI. An analysis note by Andrew Grant.

(2020b). How to waste over half a trillion dollars: The economics implications of deflationary renewable energy for coal power investment, https://carbontracker.org/reports/how-to-waste-over-half-a-trillion-dollars/.

Carcagane, S. (2019). Pays exportateurs d´hydrocarbures, les grands perdants de la transition energétique? Revue internationale et stratégique, 1(113): 119–131.

Cardoso, A. (2015). Behind the life cycle of coal: Socio-environmental liabilities of coal mining in Cesar, Colombia. Ecological Economics, 120: 71–82.

Carney, M. 2015). Breaking the tragedy of the horizon: Climate change and financial stability. Bank of England. Speech given by Mark Carney, Lloyd's of London, 29 September.

(2016). Resolving the Climate Paradox. Text of the Arthur Burns Memorial Lecture, Berlin, 22 September 2016, .www.bis.org/review/r160926h.pdf

(2019). Fifty shades of green: The world needs a new, sustainable financial system. Finance & Development (December): 12–15.

CEPAL. (2019). Panorama Social de América Latina. Naciones Unidas: Comisión Económica para América Latina y el Caribe. Santiago de Chile.

Chancel, L., & Piketty, T. (2015). Carbon and inequality: From Kyoto to Paris Trends in the global inequality of carbon emissions (1998–2013) & prospects for an equitable adaptation fund. Paris School of Economics.

Chen, G. C., & Lees C. (2016). Growing China's renewables sector: A developmental state approach. New Political Economy, 21(6): 574–86

Chenet, H., Ryan-Collins J., & van Lerven F. (2019). Climate-related financial policy in a world of radical uncertainty: Towards a precautionary approach. UCL Institute for Innovation and Public Purpose, Working Paper WP 019/13.

Cheng, I-H. – & Xiong, W. (2013). The Financialization of Commodity Markets. National Bureau of Economic Research – NBER 19642.

Chichilsnky, G., & Heal, G. (1994). Who should abate carbon emissions: an international viewpoint. National Bureau of Economic Research – NBER 4428.

Chichilnisky G., Heal, G., & Starrett, D (2000). Equity and Efficiency in Environmental Markets: Global Trade in Carbon Dioxide Emissions. In: Graciela Chichilnisky, Geoffrey Heal. (eds). Environmental Markets: Equity and Efficiency 2000. New York, Columbia University Press.

Chien, K-h. (2019) Pacing for renewable energy development: The developmental state in Taiwan's offshore wind power. Annals of the American Association of Geographers, 0(0): 1–15.

Christophers, B. (2017).Climate change and financial instability: Risk disclosure and the problematics of neoliberal governance, Annals of the American Association of Geographers, 107(5): 1108–1127, DOI:10.1080/ 24694452.2017.1293502,www.tandfonline.com/doi/full/10.1080 /24694452.2017.1293502.

Ciplet, D., & Roberts, J. T. (2017). Splintering South: Ecologically unequal exchange theory in a fragmented global climate. Journal of World-System Research, 23(2): 372–398

Clayton, B., & Levi, M. (2015). Fiscal breakeven oil prices: Uses, abuses, and opportunities for improvement. Council on Foreign Relations

Codato, D., Pappalardoa, S.E., Diantinib, A., Ferrareseb, F., Gianolia, F., & De Marchia, M. (2019). Oil production, biodiversity conservation and indigenous territories: Towards geographical criteria for unburnable carbon areas in the Amazon rainforest. Applied Geography, 102(28): 38.

Combet, E., & Méjean A. (2017) The equity and efficiency trade-off of carbon tax revenue recycling: A reexamination mimeo / available at http://www2 .centre-cired.fr/IMG/pdf/main-3.pdf (accessed on september 9th, 2020).

Cœuré, B. (2018). Monetary policy and climate change. European Bank Speech by Benoît Cœuré, Member of the Executive Board of the ECB, at a conference on "Scaling up Green Finance: The Role of Central Banks", organised by the Network for Greening the Financial System, the Deutsche Bundesbank, and the Council on Economic Policies, Berlin, 8 November 2018.

Collier, P., & Venables A. (2014). Closing coal: economic and moral incentives. University of Oxford. OxCarre Research Paper 132.

Couture, T., & Gagnon Y. (2010). An analysis of feed-in tariff remuneration models: Implications for renewable energy investment. Energy Policy, 38: 955–965.

Covert, T., Greenstone, M., & Knittel, C. R. (2016). Will we ever stop using fossil fuels? Journal of Economic Perspectives, 30(1 Winter): 117–138.

CPI (2019). Global Landscape of Climate Finance 2019. [Barbara Buchner, Alex Clark, Angela Falconer, Rob Macquarie et al.]. Climate Policy Initiative, London, https://climatepolicyinitiative.org/publication/global-landscape-of-climate-finance-2019/.

Cremer, H., Gahvari, F., & Ladoux N. (1998). Externalities and optimal taxation. Journal of Public Economics, 70: 343–364.

(2003). Environmental taxes with heterogeneous consumers: an application to energy consumption in France. Journal of Public Economics, Elsevier, 87(12): 2791–2815, December.

Christianson, G., Lee, A., Larsen, G., & Green, A. (2017). Financing the energy transition: Whether World Bank, IFC, and ADB energy supply investments are supporting a low-carbon, sustainable future. Working Paper. Washington, DC: World Resources Institute. www.wri.org/publication/ financing-the-energy-transition.

Cui, R. Y, Hultman, N., Edwards, M. R., et al. (2019). Quantifying operational lifetimes for coal power plants under the Paris goals. Nature Communications, 10.

Cust, J., Manley, D., & Cecchinato, G. (2017). Unburnable wealth of nations. Finance and Development, 54(1).

Dafe, F., & Volz, U. (2015). Financing global development: The role of central banks. German Development Institute / DeutschesInstitutfürEntwicklungspolitik (DIE).

Dale, S., & Dikau, S. (2017). Peak oil demand and long-run oil prices. British Petroleum – BP.

Dasgupta, P., Heal. G., & Stiglitz, J. (1980). The taxation of exhaustible resources. National Bureau of Economic Research – NBER Working Paper 436.

Davis, S. J., Caldeira, K., & Matthews, D. (2010). Future CO_2 emissions and climate change from existing energy infrastructure. Science, 329.

Davis S. J., & Diffenbaugh, N. (2016). Dislocated interests and climate change. Environmental Research Letters.

DeAngelis, K., & Tucker, B. (2020). Adding fuel to the fire: Export credit agencies and fossil fuel finance. Oil Change International – Friends of the Earth US.

Deaton, A. (2020). We may not all be equal in the eyes of coronavirus. *Financial Times*. April 5.

Dent, C. (2014). Renewable energy in East Asia: Towards a new developmentalism. Routledge, Taylor & Francis Group.

Devarajan, S., Goy, D. S., Robinsonz, S., & Thierfelderet, K. (2011). Tax policy to reduce carbon emissions in a distorted economy: Illustrations from a South Africa CGE model. The B.E. Journal of Economic Analysis & Policy, 11(1), Article 13.

Douenne, T. (2019). Les effets de la fiscalité écologique sur le pouvoir d'achat des ménages : simulation de plusieurs scénarios de redistribution. Conceil d'analyse economique – FOCUS, 30.

D'Orazio, P., & Popoyan, L. (2018). Fostering green investments and tackling climate-related financial risks: which role for macroprudential policies? Ruhr Economic Papers, No. 778, ISBN 978–3-86788–906-3, RWI – Leibniz-Institut für Wirtschaftsforschung, Essen, http://dx.doi.org/10.4419/86788906.

Dyllick, T., & Muff K. (2017). What does sustainability for business really mean? And when is a business truly sustainable? In S. Jeanrenaud, J. Gosling, & J. P. Jeanrenaud (eds.), Sustainable Business: A One Planet Approach. Wiley.

ECLAC. 2014a. Indigenous people's rights in Latin America: Progress in the past decade and remaining challenges. United Nations, Santiago.

2014b. The economics of climate change in Latin America and the Caribbean: Paradoxes and challenges. sustainable development and human settlements division of the economic commission for Latin America and the Caribbean – Report L. Galindo and J. Samaniego (Coor.).

2016. The Social Inequality Matrix in Latin America. A document presented at the First meeting of the Presiding Officers of the Regional Conference on Social Development in Latin America and the Caribbean; Santo Domingo, 1 November.

(2018). Economics of Climate Change in Latin America and the Caribbean: A Graphic View. Report by A. Bárcena, J. Samaniego, L. M. Galindo, J. Ferrer, J. E. Alatorre, P. Stockins, O. Reyes, L. Sánchez, & J. Mostacedo, United Nations, Santiago.

Edenhofer, O., Steckel, J.C., Jakob, M., & Bertram, C. (2018). Reports of coal's terminal decline may be exaggerated. Environ. Res. Lett. 13, 024019. https://doi.org 10.1088/1748–9326/aaa3a2.

Erickson, P., Kartha, S., Lazarus, M., & Tempest, K. (2015). Assessing carbon lock-in. Environmental Research Letters.

Fekete, H., Röser F., & Hagemann M. (2020). Aligning multilateral development banks' operations with the Paris Agreement's mitigation objectives: Raising the game on Paris Alignment. A memo series by Germanwatch, NewClimate Institute, and World Resources Institute.

Feron, S., Baigorrotegui, G., Parker, C., Opazo, J., & Cordero, R. (2018). Consumer (co-) ownership in renewables in Chile. In Jens Lowitzsch (ed.), Energy transition: Financing consumer co-ownership in renewables. Palgrave Macmillan 559–584.

Finer, M., Jenkins, C.N., Pimm, S. L., Keane, B., & Ross, C. (2008). Oil and gas projects in the Western Amazon: Threats to wilderness, biodiversity, and Indigenous Peoples. PLos One, 3(8).

Finley-Brook, M., & Holloman, E. L. (2016). Empowering energy justice. International Journal of Environmental Research and Public Health volume 13 (9).

Fischer, P., & Alexander, K. (2019). Climate change: the role for central banks. King's Business College. Data Analytics for Finance & MacroResearch Centre Working paper No. 2019/6.

Fleurbaey, M., & Zuber, S. (2013). Climate policies deserves a negative discount rate. Chicago International Journal of Law, 13(2): 565–595.

Fouquet, R. (2010), The slow search for solutions: Lessons from historical energy transitions by sector and service. Energy Policy, 38(11): 6586–6596.

(2016). Historical energy transitions: Speed, prices and system transformation. Energy Research & Social Science, 22: 7–12.

Foxon, T. J. (2002). Technological and institutional 'lock-in' as a barrier to sustainable innovation. ICCEPT Working Paper. www.imperial.ac.uk /media/imperial-college/research-centres-and-groups/icept/7294726.PDF.

Friedman, M. (1970). The Social Responsibility of Business is to increase its profits. The New York Times Magazine.

Friends of the Earth. (2017). Tackling climate change: Keeping coal, oil and gas in the ground. Briefing.

Frisari, G., Gallardo, M., Nakano, C., Cardenas, V., & Monnin P. (2019). Climate risks and financial systems of Latin America: Regulatory, supervisory and industry practices in the region and beyond. Inter-American Development Bank – IDB Technical Note 1823.

FT (2020a). Oil price turmoil reveals depths of economic pain. *Financial Times*, The Editorial Board April 21.

(2020b) Virus lays bare the frailty of the social contract: Radical reforms are required to forge a society that will work for all. *Financial Times*, The Editorial Board. April 3.

Galaz, V. (2020). Presentation at SEI WEBINAR, April 3

Gallucci, M. (2019) Energy equity: Bringing solar power to low-income communities. Yale Environment 360

Gersbach, H., & Rochet, J.C. (2017). Capital regulation and credit fluctuations. Journal of Monetary Economics, 90: 113–124.

Gerlagh, R. (2011) Too much oil. CESifo Economic Studies, 57, 79–102.

GEF. (2017). Renewable energy auctions in Latin America and the Caribbean. H. Lucas & J. C. Gomez. Global Environment Facility & Factor.

Giljum, S. (2004). Trade, materials flows, and economic development in the South: The example of Chile. Journal of Industrial Ecology, 8: 241–261.

Giljum, S., & Eisenmenger, N. (2004). North-South trade and the distribution of environmental goods and burdens: A biophysical perspective. Journal of Environment and Development, 13: 73–100.

Giljum, S., Dittrich, M., Lieber, M., & Lutter, S. (2014). Global patterns of material flows and their socio-economic and environmental implications: A MFA study on all countries world-wide from 1980 to 2009. Resources, 3: 319–339, doi:10.3390/resources3010319.

Givens, J. E., Huang, X., & Jorgenson, A. K. (2019). Ecologically unequal exchange: A theory of global environmental injustice. Sociology Compass.

Goldthau, A., & Sovacool, B. (2012). The uniqueness of the energy security, justice, and governance problem. Energy Policy, 41: 232–240.

Gómez Sabaini, J.C., Jiménez, J.P., & Moran, D. (2017). "El impacto fiscal de los recursos naturales no renovables" Chapter XIV (393–414). In "Juan Carlos Gómez Sabaini, Juan Pablo Giménez, and Ricardo Martner editores "Consensos y conflictos en la política tributaria de América Latina". Comisión Económica para América Latina y el Caribe – Cooperación Española

González-Mahecha, E., Lecuyer, O., Halack, M., Basilean, M., & Vogt-Schilb, A. (2019). Committed emissions and the risk of stranded assets from power plants in Latin America and the Caribean. Inter-Ameircan Development bank – Climate Change Division. Discussion Paper 108-DP–00708.

Gramkow, C., Brandão da Silva Simões, P., & Kreimerman, R. (2020). O grande impulso (big push) energético do Uruguai. Escritorio da CEPAL em Brasilia – Serie Estudos e Perspectiva.

Griffith-Jones, S., Attridge, S., & Gouett, M. (2020). Securing climate finance through national development banks. Overseas Development Institute – ODI Report.

Gunningham, N. (2013) Managing the energy trilemma: The case of Indonesia. Energy Policy, Elsevier, 54(C): 184–193.

Habermas, J. (1984). "The theory of communicative action" Boston Beacon Press.

Haldane, A. (2011). The short long. 29th société universitaire europáeene de recherches financiáres colloquium: New paradigms in money and finance? Brussels. Technical report, Bank of England.

 (2013). Why institutions matter (more than ever). In Speech delivered at Centre for Research on Socio-Cultural Change (CRESC) Annual Conference, School of Oriental and African Studies, London, www.bankofengland.co.uk /speech/2013/why-institutions-matter-now-more-than-ever.

Halstead, M., Donker, J., Dalla Longa, F., & van der Zwaan, B. (2018). The importance of finance for Europe's Energy Transition. Energy Transition Studies.

Hansen, J., & Sato, M. (2016). Regional climate change and national responsibilities. Environmental Research Letters.

Hansen, U. E., Nygaard, I., Morris, M., & Robbins, G. (2019). Local content requirements in auction schemes for renewable energy: Enabler of local industrial development in developing countries? UNEP DTU Partnership Working Paper Series 2017, Vol. 2.

Harari, Y. N. (2020). The world after coronavirus. *Financial Times*.

Harstad, B. (2012). Buy Coal! A case for supply-side environmental policy. Journal of Political Economy 120(1): 77–115.

Hart, O., & Zingales L. (2017). Companies Should Maximize Shareholder Welfare Not Market Value? Journal of Law, Finance, and Accounting, 2: 247–274

Heal, G., & Schlenker, W. (2019). Coase, Hotelling and Pigou: The incidence of a carbon tax and C02 emissions. National Bureau of Economic Research – NBER Working Paper Series 26086

Heffron, R. J., McCauley, D., & Sovacool B. (2015). Resolving society's energy trilemma through the Energy Justice Metric. Energy Policy 87: 168–176.

Hirth, L., & Steckel J. C. (2016). The role of capital costs in decarbonizing the electricity sector. Environmental Research Letters, https://iopscience .iop.org/article/10.1088/1748–9326/11/11/114010.

Holstenkamp, L. (2018). Financing Consumer (Co-)ownership of Renewable Energy Sources. In Jens Lowitzsch (ed.), Energy Transition Financing Consumer Co-ownership in Renewables. Palgrave Macmillan: 115–138.

Hsiang, S., Oliva, P. & Walkeret, R. (2018). The distribution of Environmental Damages. National Bureau of Economic Research. NBER Working Paper Series 23882

IEA (2017). Energy Access Outlook 2017: From Poverty to Prosperity. International Energy Agency – World Energy Outlook Special Report.

IIF Capital Flows Tracker, April 2020. The COVID-19 Cliff. The International Institute of Finance.

IISD (2019). Compensation under investment treaties. International Institute for Sustainable Development – IISD Best Practices Series, October (retrieved March 26, 2020), www.iisd.org/sites/default/files/publications/compensa tion-treaties-best-practicies-en.pdf.

IMF (2019). Fiscal Monitor: How to Mitigate Climate Change. International Monetary Fund. Washington, DC.

IPCC (2007). Climate Change 2007: Synthesis Report. Contribution of Working Groups I, II and III to the Fourth Assessment Report of the Intergovernmental Panel on Climate Change. Geneva, Switzerland: IPCC. www.ipcc.ch/site/assets/uploads/2018/03/ar4_wg2_full_report.pdf.

(2012). Renewable Energy Sources and Climate Change Mitigation. Special Report of the Intergovernmental Panel on Climate Change. Summary for Policy Makers and Technical Summary.

(2018). Summary for Policymakers. In Global Warming of 1.5°C. An IPCC Special Report on the Impacts of Global Warming of 1.5°C above Pre-Industrial Levels and Related Global Greenhouse Gas Emission Pathways, in the Context of Strengthening the Global Response To the Threat of Climate Change. Geneva, Switzerland: IPCC.

IRENA (2013). Renewable Energy Auctions in Developing Countries. International Renewable Energy Agency – A report by Hugo Lucas, Rabia Ferroukhi and Diala Hawila.

(2014). Renewable Energy Market Analysis. Latin America. International Renewable Energy Agency. Abu Dhabi.

(2019a). Renewable Energy Statistics 2019. International Renewable Energy Agency. Abu Dhabi.

(2019b). A New World: The Geopolitics of the Energy Transformation. International Renewable Energy Agency. Abu Dhabi.

Jaakkola, N. (2012). Green technologies and the protracted end to the age of oil: A strategic analysis. Research Paper 99, OxCarre, Department of Economics, University of Oxford.

Jacobs, B. & Ploeg, F. van der (2019). Redistribution and pollution taxes with non-linear Engel curves. Journal of Environmental Economics and Management 95: 198–226

Jacobs, D., & Sovacool B. (2012). Feed-In Tariffs and Other Support Mechanisms for Solar PV Promotion. In Wilfried van Sark and Larry Kazmerski (eds.), Comprehensive Renewable Energy, vol. 1, p. 73–109. Elsevier.

Jacobs, D., Marzolf, N., Paredes, J.R., Rickerson, W., Flynn, H., Becker-Birk, C., & Solana Peralta, M. (2013). Analysis of renewable energy incentives in the Latin America and Caribbean region: The feed-in tariff case. Energy Policy, 60: 601–610.

Jaffe, A. M. (2020). Striking oil ain't what it used to be: Poor countries find fossil fuels just as the rich world swears them off. Foreign Affairs, January 20th.

Kalamova, M., Kaminker C., & Johnstone N. (2011). Sources of Finance, Investment Policies and Plant Entry in the Renewable Energy Sector. Organisation for Economic Co-operation and Development. OECD Environment Working Papers No. 37.

Kim, S.-Y. & Thurbon E. (2015). Developmental environmentalism: Explaining South Korea's ambitious pursuit of green growth. Politics & Society, 43(2) 213–240.

Klenert, D., Mattauch, L., Combet, E., Edenhofer, O., Hepburn, C., Rafaty, R. & Stern, N. (2018). Making carbon pricing work for citizens. Nature Climate Change 8(8): 669–677.

Knot, K. (2018). From mission to supervision: Keynote speech by Klaas Knot at the Bundesbank Symposium 'Banking supervision in dialogue' Frankfurt, 7 March 2018.

Krogstrup, S., & Oman, W. (2019). Macroeconomic and financial policies for climate change mitigation: A review of the literature. International Monetary Fund. IMF Working Paper WP/19/85.

Kunreuther, H., Heal, G., Allen, M., Edenhofer, O, Field, C. B., & Yohe, G. (2012). Risk management and climate change. National Bureau for Economic Research – NBER Working Paper 18607.

Kuntze, J.-C. & Moerenhout T. (2013). Local content requirements and the renewable energy industry: A good match? International Centre for Trade and Sustainable Development (ICTSD). International Environment House 27 Chemin de Balexert, 1219 Geneva, Switzerland

Lanier, J., and Weyl, E. G. (2020). How civic technology can help stop a pandemic: Taiwan's initial success is a model for the rest of the world. Foreign Affairs.

Lapachelle, E., MacNeil, R., & Paterson, M. (2017). The political economy of decarbonisation: From green energy 'race' to green 'division of labour'. New Political Economy, 22:3, 311–327, DOI:10.1080/13563467.2017.1240669.

Larrea, C., & Murmis M. A. (2018). Unburnable carbon and biodiversity: A global fund for keeping fossil fuels in the ground in biodiversity hotspots of developing countries. Paper presented at the Second International Conference on Fossil Fuel Supply and Climate Policy – The Queen's College, Oxford. 24–25 September 2018.

Liebrich. COVID – 19: The Low Carbon Crisis. March 26, 2020 https://about.bnef.com/blog/covid-19-the-low-carbon-crisis/

Lenton, T. M., Held, H., Kriegler, E., Hall, J. W., Lucht, W., Rahmstorf, S., and Schellnhuber, H. J. (2008). Tipping elements in the Earth's climate system. Proceedings of the National Academy of Sciences, 105: 1786–1793

Lessman, J., Fajardo, J., Muñoz, J., & Bonaccorso, E. (2016). Large expansion of oil industry in the Ecuadorian Amazon: Biodiversity vulnerability and conservation alternatives. Ecology and Evolution, 6(14): 4997–5012.

LeQuesne, T. (2019). From Carbon Democracy to Carbon Rebellion: Countering Petro-Hegemony on the Frontlines of Climate Justice. Journal of World-Systems Research, 25(1): 15–27.

Levine, S. (2015). The Powerhouse: Inside the invention of a battery to save the world. Viking–The Penguin Group

Lewis, J. (2011). Building a national wind turbine industry: Experiences from China, India and South Korea. International Journal of Technology and Globalisation, 5(3/4).

Lilliestam J., Labordena, M., Patt A., & Pfenninger, S. (2017). Empirically observed learning rates for concentrating solar power and their responses to regime change. Nature Energy, 2.

Lo, A. W. (2017). Adaptative markets: Financial evolution at the speed of thought. Princeton University Press.

Loorbach, D., Frantzeskaki, N., & Avelino, F. (2017). Sustainability Transitions Research: Transforming Science and Practice for Societal Change. Annual Review of Environment and Resources 42(1) DOI:10.1146/annurev-environ-102014-021340.

López, R. (2010). Structural adjustment and sustainable development. Initiative for Policy Dialogue (IPD) – Task Force on Environmental Economics. Working Paper Series.

Lowitzsch, J. (2018a). Introduction: The Challenge of achieving the energy transition. In Jens Lowitzsch (ed.), Energy transition Financing consumer co-ownership in renewables. Palgrave Macmillan: 1–26.

(2018b). The Consumer at the Heart of the Energy Markets. In Jens Lowitzsch (ed.), Energy transition: Financing consumer co-ownership in renewables. Palgrave Macmillan: 59–77.

Lutter, F.S., Stefan G., & Bruckner, M. (2016) A review and comparative assessment of existing approaches to calculate material footprints. Ecological Economics, 127.

Mainhart, H. (2019). World Bank Group Financial Flows undermine the Paris Climate Agreement: The WBG contributes to higher profit margins for oil, gas, and coal. URGEWORLD Organization (available at https://urgewald .org/sites/default/files/World_Bank_Fossil_Projects_WEB.pdf).

McCauley, D., & Heffron, R. (2018). Just transition: Integrating climate, energy and environmental justice. Energy Policy, 119: 1–7.

Malcomson, S. (2020). How China became the world's leader in green energy and what decoupling could cost the environment. Foreign Affairs, March-April.

Manley, D., Cust, J., & Cecchinato, G. (2017). Stranded nations? The Climate Policy implications for fossil fuel-rich developing countries. Oxford – Department of Economics, Oxford Centre for the Analysis of Resource Rich Economies – OxCarre Policy Paper 34.

Manley, D., Cust, J. & Cecchinato, G., Mihalyi, D., & Heller, P. (2019). Hidden giants: It's time for more transparency in the management and governance of national oil companies. Finance and Development – December.

Martin, P. L., & Scholz I. (2014). Policy debate | Ecuador's Yasuní-ITT Initiative: What can we learn from its failure? Revue Internationale de Politique de Développement 5(2), https://doi.org/10.4000/poldev.1705.

Masini, A., & Menichetti, E., 2012. The impact of behavioral factors in the renewable energy investment decision making process: conceptual framework and empirical findings. Energy Policy 40: 28–38.

Mazzucato, M. (2013). The entrepreneurial state: dDebunking public vs. private sector myths. Anthem Press.

(2015). The green entrepreneurial state. In I. Scoones, M. Leach, and P. Newell (ed.), The politics of green transformations, pp. 134–52. Routledge.

Mazzucato, M., & Semieniuk, G. (2018). Financing renewable energy: Who is financing what and why it matters. Technological Forecasting & Social Change, 127: 8–22

McGlade, C., & Ekins, P. (2015). The geographical distribution of fossil fuels unused when limiting global warming to 20C. Nature 187 – Letter.

McKibbin, W. J., Morris, A., & Wilcoxen P. T. (2008). Expecting the unexpected: Macroeconomic volatility and climate policy. The Harvard Project on International Climate Agreements. Discussion Paper 08–16.

Meadows, D. H., Meadows, D. L., Randers, J., & Behrens, W. W. (1972). The limits to growth. Universe Books.

Mehling M. A., van Asselt, H., Das, K., Droege, S., & Verkuijl, C. (2019). Designing border carbon adjustments for enhanced climate action. The American Journal of International Law, 113(3): 433–481.

Mena, C. F., Arsel, M., Pellegrini, L., et al. (2019): Community-based monitoring of oil extraction: Lessons learned in the Ecuadorian Amazon. Society & Natural Resources, DOI:10.1080/08941920.2019.1688441.

Mercure, J., Pollitt, H., Vinuales, J., et al. (2018) Macroeconomic impact of stranded fossil fuel assets in Nature Climate Change 8: 588–593.

Mignon, I., & Rüdinger, A. (2016) The impact of systemic factors on the deployment of cooperative projects within renewable electricity production: An international comparison. Renewable and Sustainable Energy Reviews, 65: 478–488, http://dx.doi.org/10.1016/j.rser.2016.07.026.

Minsky, H. (2008). Stabilizing an unstable economy. McGraw Hill.

Mitchell, T. (2009). Carbon democracy. Economy and Society 38(3): 399–432.

Morris, A. (2016). The challenge of state reliance on revenue from fossil fuel production. Brookings – The Climate and Energy Economics Projects. Climate and Energy Economics Discussion Paper.

Mukand, S., & Rodrik, D. (2015). The political economy of liberal democracy. National Bureau for Economic Research – NBER Working Paper 21540.

Muñoz P., Giljum, S. & Rocaet, J. (2009). The Raw Material Equivalents of International Trade Empirical Evidence for Latin America. Journal of Industrial Ecology Volume 13, Issue 6.

Muradian R., Walter, M., & Martinez-Alier, J. (2012). Hegemonic transitions and global shifts in social metabolism: Implications for resource-rich countries. Introduction to the special section. Global Environmental Change.

Nelson, D. (2018). Energy transition: the greatest switch capital markets have ever seen. Climate Policy Initiative (CPI) Energy Finance. http://climate change-theneweconomy.com/energy-transition-greatest-switch-capital-markets-ever-seen/.

Newell, P., & Mulaney, D. (2013). The political economy of the 'just transition. The Geographical Journal Volume 179, Issue 2: 132–140.

Newig, J., and Karda, E. (2012). Participation in environmental governance: legitimate and effective? In Karl Hogl, Eva Kvarda, Ralf Nordbeck, and Michael Pregernig (eds.), Environmental Governance: The Challenge of Legitimacy and Efectiveness. Edgar Elgar Publishers: 29–45.

Noboa, E., & Upham, P. (2018). Energy policy and transdisciplinary transition management arenas in illiberal democracies: A conceptual framework. Energy Research & Social Science, 46: 114–124.

Nordhaus, W. (1973). The Allocation of Energy Reserves. Brookings Papers 3, 529–570.

.(2008). A question of balance: Weighing the options on global warming policies. Yale University Press.

(2020). How to fix a failing global effort. Foreign Affairs, April.

Nussbaum, M. (2018). Monarchy of fear: A philosopher looks at our political crisis. Simon & Schuster.

Ocampo, J.A. (2011). The transition to a green economy: Benefits, challenges and risks from a sustainable development perspective. Prepared under the direction of: Division for Sustainable Development, UN-DESA United Nations Environment Programme UN Conference on Trade and Development.

Ocampo, J. A., Rada, C., & Taylor, L. (2009). Growth and policy in developing countries: A structuralist approach. Initiative for Policy Dialogue at Columbia University – Columbia University Press.

ODI – OCI (2015). Empty promises: G20 subsidies to oil, gas and coal production. A report prepared by Elizabeth Bast, Alex Doukas, Sam Pickard, Laurie van der Burg and Shelagh Whitley. Overseas Development Institute – Oil Change International, www.odi.org/publica tions/10058-empty-promises-g20-subsidies-oil-gas-and-coal-production.

OECD (2013). The climate challenge: Achieving zero emissions. Lecture by the OECD Secretary-General, Mr. Angel Gurría. London, 9 October, www .oecd.org/about/secretary-general/the-climate-challenge-achieving-zero-emissions.htm.

(2019). ESTADÍSTICAS TRIBUTARIAS EN AMÉRICA LATINA Y EL CARIBE . Publicación conjunta: OCDE – DEV, Centro de Desarrollo. BID. CEPAL Naciones Unidas. Centro Interamericano de administraciones tributarias – CIAT.

Oil Change International (2017). Talk is cheap: How G20 governments are financing climate disaster. Oil Change International, Friends of the Earth U.S., the Sierra Club, and WWF European Policy Office

Ondraczek, J., Nadejda, K., & Patt, A .G. (2013) WACC the dog: The effect of financing costs on the levelized cost of solar pv power. Renewable Energy, 75, March 2015, http://dx.doi.org/10.2139/ssrn.2321130.

O'Sullivan, M., Overland, I., & Sandalow, D. (2017). The geopolitics of renewable energy. Columbia SIPA Center on Global Energy Policy – Harvard Kennedy School Belfer Center for Science and International Affairs – Norewgian Institute for International Affairs. Working Paper.

Pérez-Rincon, M. A. (2006). colombian international trade from a physical perspective: Towards a "prebish thesis". Ecological Economics.

Peters, G. P., Minx, J. C., Weber, C. L., & Edenhofer, O. (2011). Growth in emission transfers via international trade from 1990 to 2008. PNAS, 108: 21.

Pfeiffer, J. (2017). Fossil resources and climate change: the green paradox and resource market power revisited in general equilibrium. IFO Institut

Pfeiffer, A., Hepburn, C., Vogt-Schilb, A., & Caldecott, B. (2018). Committed emissions from existing and planned power plants and asset stranding required to meet the Paris Agreement. Environmental Research Letters 13, https://doi.org/10.1088/1748–9326/aabc5f.

Pickl, M.J. (2019). The renewable energy strategies of oil majors: From oil to energy? Energy Strategy Reviews, 26: 100370

Pigott, G., Boyland, M., Down, A., & Raluca Torre, A. (2019). Realizing a just and equitable transition away from fossil fuels. Stockholm Environment Institute – SEI Brief Discussion.

Piketty, T. (2014). Capital in the twenty-first century. Harvard University Press. (2020). Capital e Ideología. Paidós.

Ploeg, F. van der, & Withagen, C. A. M. (2012). Is there really a green paradox? Journal of Environmental Economics and Management.

(2015). Global warming and the green paradox: A review of adverse effects of climate policies. Review of Environmental Economics and Policy, 9(2): 285–303.

Ploeg, F. van der, & Rezai, A. (2018). Climate policy and stranded carbon assets: A financial perspective. OxCarre Working Papers 206, Oxford

Centre for the Analysis of Resource Rich Economies, University of Oxford.

Pond, A. (2017). Financial liberalization: Stable autocracies and constrained democracies. Comparative Political Studies, 51(1): 105–135.

Przeworski, A. (2010) Consensus, conflict, and compromise in western thought on representative government. Procedia: Social and Behavioral Sciences 2 (5): 7042–7055.

Ragazzoni D. (2018). Political compromise in party democracy: An overlooked puzzle in Kelsen's democratic theory. In Christian Rostboll & Theresa Scavenius (eds.), Compromise and disagreement in contemporary political theory. Routledge: 95–112.

Rainforest Action Network (2019). Banking on climate change: Fossil fuel report 2019. A joint publication of Oil Change International – BankTrack – Rainforest Action Network – Sierra Club, www.ran.org/bank ingonclimatechange2019/.

Rajan, R. (2019). The third pillar: How markets and the state leave the community behind. Penguin Books.

Ray, R., Gallagher, K., López, A., & Sanborn, C. (2017). China and sustainable development in Latin America: The social and environmental dimension. Anthem Frontiers on Global Political Economy:Anthem Press.

Ripple, W. J., Wolf, C., Newsome, T. M., Barnard, P., & Moomaw W. R. (2020). World scientists' warning of a climate emergency, BioScience, 70(1, January 2020), 8–12, https://doi.org/10.1093/biosci/biz088.

Robinson, M., and Reddy, D. (2020). Tackling climate change with COVID-19 urgency. Project Syndicate.

Rosenbloom, D. (2017). Pathways: An emerging concept for the theory and governance of low-carbon transitions. Global Environmental Change, 43: 37–50.

Rudebusch, G. D. (2019). Climate change and the Federal Reserve. FRBSF Economic Letter 2019–09 | March 25, 2019 | Research from the Federal Reserve Bank of San Francisco

Runney, G. (2019). Shared journey, different choices: Will Latin America realize its energy future? EY. 22/05/2019.

Samaniego, P., Vallejo, M. C., & Martinez-Allier, J. (2017). Commercial and biophysical deficits in South America, 1990–2013. Ecological Economics, 133: 62–73.

Sandin, L. (2020). COVID-19 exposes Latin America's inequality. Center for Strategic & International Studies – Commentary, www.csis.org/analysis/covid-19-exposes-latin-americas-inequality.

San Sebastian, M. & Hurtig, A.K. (2004). Oil exploitation in the Amazon basin of Ecuador: a public health emergency. Revista Panamericana de Salud Pública / Public Health 15 (3).

Sauvant, K., & Mann H. (2017). Towards an indicative list of FDI sustainability characteristics. ICTSD and WEF – E15 Task Force: Strengthening the Global Trade and Investment System for Sustainable Development.

Schaffartzik, A., Mayer, A., Gingrich, S., Eisenmenger, N., Loy, C., & Krausman F. (2014). The global metabolic transition: Regional patterns and trends of global material flows, 1950–2010. Global Environmental Change, 26: 87–97.

Schaffitzel, F., Jakob, M., Soria, R., Vogt-Schilb, R., & Ward R. (2019). Can government transfers make energy subsidy reform socially acceptable? A case study on Ecuador. InterAmerican Development Bank – IDB Working Paper Series N ° IDB-WP-01026.

Scheffer, M., Carpenter, S., Foley, J. A., Folke, C., & Walker, B. (2001). Catastrophic shifts in ecosystems. Nature, 413: 591–596.

Scheidel, W. (2017). The great leveler: Violence and the history of inequality from the Stone Age to the twenty-first century. Princeton University Press.

Schmidt, T. S.; Born, R., & Schneider, M. (2012). Assessing the costs of photovaltaic and wind power in six developing countries. Nature Climate Change, 2(7): 548–553.

Schoenmaker, D., & Schramade, W. (2019). Principles of sustainable finance. Oxford University Press.

Schumpeter, Joseph A. 1942. Capitalism, socialism, and democracy. New York: Harper&Brothers.

Sen, A. (2020). A better society can emerge from the lockdowns. *Financial Times*. Opinion.

Sester, B., & Frank, C. V. (2017). Using external breakeven prices to track vulnerabilities in oil-exporting countries. Council on Foreign Relations.

Seto, K. C., Davis, S., Mitchell R., Stokes E., Unruh, G., & Urge-Vorsatz, D. (2016). Carbon lock-in: Types, causes, and policy implications. Annual Reviews Environmental Resources. 41(19): 1–19, www.annualreviews.org/doi/abs/10.1146/annurev-environ–110615–085934.

Shapira, R., & Zingales L. (2017). Is pollution value – Maximizing? The Dupont Case. National Bureau of Economic Research – NBER Working Paper 23866.

Sinn, H.-W. (2008). Public policies against global warming: A supply side approach. International Tax Public Finance 15: 360–394.

Sinnott, E., Nash, J., & de la Torre, A. (2010). Natural resources in Latin America and the Caribbean: Beyond booms and busts? The World Bank. Washington, DC.

Smith, P., & Sells, C. (2016). Democracy in Latin America. Oxford University Press. 3rd ed.

Solimano, A. (2012). Chile and the Neoliberal trap: The post-Pinochet era. Cambridge University Press.

(2015). Crecimiento, Desigualdad y Democracia: La Transformación Capitalista en Chile. In R. Cordera, M. Flores, & M. L. Fuentes, (eds.), México Social: Regresar a lo Fundamental UNAM, México.

Solt, F. (2008). Economic inequality and democratic political engagement. American Journal of Political Science. 52(1): 48–60.

Sonnenfeld D. A., & Leigh Taylor, P. (2018). Liberalism, illiberalism, and the environment. Society & Natural Resources, 31(5): 515–524.

Sovacool, B. K. (2016). 'How long will it take?' Conceptualizing the temporal dynamics of energy transitions. Energy Research & Social Science, 13: 202–215.

Stanley, L. E. (2020). The IPE of development finance in Latin America. In Ernesto Vivares (ed.), The Routledge Handbook to Global Political Economy: Conversations and Inquiries, Routledge Press: 581–599.

Steffen, W., Richardson, K., Rockström, J., et al. (2015). Planetary boundaries: Guiding human development on a changing planet. Science. February.

Stern, N. (2007). The economics of climate change: The Stern report. Cambridge University Press.

Stevens, P. (2019). The Geopolitical Implications of Future Oil Demand. Chatman House – The Royal Institute for International Affairs. Energy, Environment and Resources Department, Research Paper.

Stiglitz, J. (2006). Making globalization work. W.W. Norton & Company.

Stiglitz, J. & Stern, N. (2017). Report of the High Level Commission on Carbon Prices. The World Bank. Washington, DC.

Stiglitz, J., Jayadev, A., & Prabhala, A. (2020). Patents versus the Pandemic. Project Syndicate, www.project-syndicate.org/commentary/covid19-drugs-and-vaccine-demand-patent-reform-by-joseph-e-stiglitz-et-al -2020–04.

Strambo, C., González Espinosa, A. C., Puertas Velasco, J. A., & Atteridge, A. (2018). Privileged coal: The politics of subsidies for coal production in Colombia. SEI – Stockholm Environment Institute, Working Paper 01.

Studart, R., & Gallagher, K. (2016). Infrastructure for sustainable development: The role of national development banks. Boston University – Global Economic Governance Initiative. GEGI Policy Brief 07/10.

Taleb, N. N., Read, R., Douady, R., Norman, J., & Bar-Yam, Y. (2014). The precautionary principle (with application to the genetic modification of organisms). Extreme Risk Initiative – New York University School of Engineering Working Paper Series, www.fooledbyrandomness.com/pp2 .pdf.

Tarhan, M. D. (2015). Renewable Energy Cooperatives: A Review of Demonstrated Impacts and Limitations. Journal of Entrepreneural and Organizational Diversity – JEOD Volume 4, Issue 1: 104–120

Thanassoulis, J. (2014). Bank pay caps, bank risk, and macroprudential regulation. Journal of Banking & Finance 48: 139–151.

Thomä, J., & Chenet, H. (2017). Transition risks and market failure: A theoretical discourse on why financial models and economic agents may misprice risk related to the transition to a low-carbon economy. Journal of Sustainable Finance & Investment. 7(1): 82–98.

Thurbon, E. (2019). The Future Of Financial Activism in Taiwan? The utility of a mindset-centred analysis of developmental states and their evolution. New Political Economy, DOI:10.1080/13563467.2018.1562436.

Therborn, G. (2012). The Killing Fields of inequality. International Journal of Health Services, 42(4): 579–589.

Tienhaara, K. (2009). The expropriation of environmental governance: Protecting foreign investors at the expense of public policy. Cambridge University Press.

Tillemann, L. (2015). The great race: The global quest for the car of the future. Simone Schuster Paperbacks.

Tragedy of the Horizon. (2017). All swans are black in the dark: How the short-term focus of financial analysis does not shed light on long term risks. Tragedy of the Horizon – A 2° Investing Initiative & Generation Foundation Project.

Tudela, F. (2018). Obstacles and opportunities for moratoria on oil/ gas exploration or extraction in Latin America & the Caribbean. Paper presented at the Second International Conference on Fossil Fuel Supply and Climate Policy – The Queen's College, Oxford. 24–25 September 2018.

UNEP. (2016). global material flows and resource productivity. Assessment report for the UNEP International Resource Panel.

Unruh, G. C. (2000). Understanding carbon lock-in. Energy Policy 28: 817–830.

van der Meijden, G., van der Ploeg, F., & Withagen, C (2015). International Capital Markets, Oil Producers and the Green Paradox. Oxford Centre for the Analysis of Resource Rich Economies OxCarre Research Paper 130.

Vera, L. (2019). Impuestos ambientales y equidad: desafíos para América Latina y el Caribe. Friederick Ebert Stitfung – FES, Analisis, http://library.fes.de/pdf-files/bueros/kolumbien/15468.pdf.

Vercelli, A. (2019). Finance and democracy: Towards a sustainable financial system. Palgrave Macmillan.

Verkuijl, C., Piggot, G., Lazarus, M., van Asselt, H., & Erickson, P. (2018). Aligning fossil fuel production with the Paris Agreement Insights for the UNFCCC Talanoa Dialogue. Stockholm Environment Institute – SEI.

Viscidi, L., & Yepez A. (2020). Clean energy auctions in Latin America. Inter-American Development Bank.

Vitale, D. (2006). Between deliberative and participatory democracy: A contribution on Habermas. Philosophy & Social Criticism, 32(6): 739–766.

Vogt- Schilb, A., Walsh, B., Feng, K., et al. (2019). Cash transfers for pro-poor carbon taxes in Latin America and the Caribbean. InterAmerican Development Bank – Climate Change Division. IDB Working Paper 1046.

Volz, U. (2017). On the role of Central Banks in enhancing green finance. UN Environment. Inquiry – Design of a Sustainable Financial System.

Waissbein, O., Glemarec, Y., Bayraktar, H., & Schmidt, T.S. (2013). Derisking renewable energy investment: A framework to support policymakers in selecting public instruments to promote renewable energy investment in developing countries. New York: United Nations Development Programme

WCED (1987). Our Common Future. Oxford: World Commission on Environment and Development, published by the United Nations through the Oxford University Press.

WEC (2018). World Energy Trilemma Index 2018, published by the World Energy Council (2018) in partnership with Oliver Wyman.

Weidman, T., Schandl, H., Lenzen, M., et al. (2013). The material footprint of nations. PNAS – Proceedings of the National Academy of Sciences, 112.

Weitzman, M. (2009). On modeling and interpreting the economics of catastrophic climate change. Review of Economics and Statistics, 91(1): 1–19.

Whitley, S. (2013). At cross-purposes: Subsidies and climate compatible investment. Overseas Development Institute – ODI, London.

Wixforth, S., & Hoffmann, R. (2019). Thinking climate and social policies as one. Social Europe, www.socialeurope.eu/thinking-climate-and-social-policies-as-one.

Wolf, M. (2020).This pandemic is an ethical challenge. *Financial Times.* 24 March 2020.

Wright, N. (2020). Coronavirus and the future of surveillance: Democracies must offer an alternative to authoritarian solutions. Foreign Affairs.

Wright, H., Holmes, I., Barbe, R., & Hawkins, J. (2017). Greening financial flows: What progress has been made in the development banks? E3G – Briefing Paper.

Yildiz, Ö. (2014). Financing renewable energy infrastructures via financial citizen participation: The case of Germany. Renewable Energy, 68: 677–685.

Yildiz, Ö., Rommelb, J., Deborc, S., et al. (2015). Renewable energy cooperatives as gatekeepers or facilitators? Recent developments in Germany and a multidisciplinary research agenda. Energy Research & Social Science, 6: 59–73.

Yuang, F., & Gallagher, K. (2018). greening development lending in the Americas: trends and determinants. Ecological Economics. Elsevier, volume 154: 189–200.

Zahno, M., & Castro, P. (2017). Renewable energy deployment at the interplay between support policies and fossil fuel subsidies. In Stefan E. Weishaar, Larry Kreiser, Janet E. Milne, Hope Ashiabor, & Michael Mehling. The green market transition: Carbon taxes, energy subsidies and smart instrument mixes, pp. 97–112. Edward Elgar.

Zarsky, L., & Stanley, L. E. (2013). Can extractive industries promote sustainable development? A net benefits framework and a case study of the Marlin Mine in Guatemala. The Journal of Environment and Development, 22(2).

Zarsky, L. (2014). From "investor rights" to "sustainable development"? Challenges and innovations in international investment rules. In David A. Deese (ed.), Handbook of the International Political Economy of Trade, Elgar Edgard.

Zakaria, F. (1997). The rise of illiberal democracy. Foreign Affairs.

Zenghelis, D. & Stern, N. (2016). The importance of looking forward to manage risks: submission to the Task Force on Climate-Related Financial Disclosures. ESRC Centre for Climate Change Economics and Policy Grantham Research Institute on Climate Change and the Environment.

Zhou L., Gilbert, S., Wang, Y., Muñoz Cabré, M., & Gallager K. (2018). Moving the Green Belt and Road Initiative: from words to actions. World Resource Institute – Global Development Policy Center. Working Paper.

Cambridge Elements ≡

Economics of Emerging Markets

Bruno S. Sergi
Harvard University

Editor Bruno S. Sergi is an Instructor at Harvard University, an Associate of the Harvard University Davis Center for Russian and Eurasian Studies and Harvard Ukrainian Research Institute. He is the Academic Series Editor of the Cambridge *Elements in the Economics of Emerging Markets* (Cambridge University Press), a co-editor of the *Lab for Entrepreneurship and Development* book series, and associate editor of *The American Economist*. Concurrently, he teaches International Economics at the University of Messina, Scientific Director of the Lab for Entrepreneurship and Development (LEAD), and a co-founder and Scientific Director of the International Center for Emerging Markets Research at RUDN University in Moscow. He has published over 150 articles in professional journals and twenty-one books as author, co-author, editor, and co-editor.

About the Series
The aim of this Elements series is to deliver state-of-the-art, comprehensive coverage of the knowledge developed to date, including the dynamics and prospects of these economies, focusing on emerging markets' economics, finance, banking, technology advances, trade, demographic challenges, and their economic relations with the rest of the world, as well as the causal factors and limits of economic policy in these markets.

Cambridge Elements $^{\equiv}$

Economics of Emerging Markets

Printed in the United States
By Bookmasters